MznLnx

Missing Links Exam Preps

Exam Prep for

College Algebra

Blitzer, 3rd Edition

The MznLnx Exam Prep is your link from the texbook and lecture to your exams.
The MznLnx Exam Preps are unauthorized and comprehensive reviews of your textbooks.

All material provided by MznLnx and Rico Publications (c) 2010
Textbook publishers and textbook authors do not particpate in or contribute to these reviews.

MznLnx

Rico Publications

Exam Prep for College Algebra
3rd Edition
Blitzer

Publisher: Raymond Houge
Assistant Editor: Michael Rouger
Text and Cover Designer: Lisa Buckner
Marketing Manager: Sara Swagger
Project Manager, Editorial Production: Jerry Emerson
Art Director: Vernon Lowerui

Product Manager: Dave Mason
Editorial Assitant: Rachel Guzmanji
Pedagogy: Debra Long
Cover Image: Jim Reed/Getty Images
Text and Cover Printer: City Printing, Inc.
Compositor: Media Mix, Inc.

(c) 2010 Rico Publications
ALL RIGHTS RESERVED. No part of this work covered by the copyright may be reproduced or used in any form or by an means--graphic, electronic, or mechanical, including photocopying, recording, taping, Web distribution, information storage, and retrieval systems, or in any other manner--without the written permission of the publisher.

For more information about our products, contact us at:
Dave.Mason@RicoPublications.com

For permission to use material from this text or product, submit a request online to:
Dave.Mason@RicoPublications.com

Printed in the United States
ISBN:

Contents

CHAPTER 1
Prerequisites: Fundamental Concepts of Alaebra — 1

CHAPTER 2
Equations, Inequalities, and Mathematical Models — 17

CHAPTER 3
Functions and Graphs — 30

CHAPTER 4
Polynomial and Rational Functions — 39

CHAPTER 5
Exponential and Logarithmic Functions — 48

CHAPTER 6
Systems of Equations and Inequalities — 53

CHAPTER 7
Matrices and Determinants — 60

CHAPTER 8
Conic Sections and Analytic Geometry — 72

CHAPTER 9
Sequences, Induction, and Probability — 78

ANSWER KEY — 88

TO THE STUDENT

COMPREHENSIVE

The *MznLnx* Exam Prep series is designed to help you pass your exams. Editors at MznLnx review your textbooks and then prepare these practice exams to help you master the textbook material. Unlike study guides, workbooks, and practice tests provided by the texbook publisher and textbook authors, *MznLnx* gives you **all** of the material in each chapter in exam form, not just samples, so you can be sure to nail your exam.

MECHANICAL

The MznLnx Exam Prep series creates exams that will help you learn the subject matter as well as test you on your understanding. Each question is designed to help you master the concept. Just working through the exams, you gain an understanding of the subject--its a simple mechanical process that produces success.

INTEGRATED STUDY GUIDE AND REVIEW

MznLnx is not just a set of exams designed to test you, its also a comprehensive review of the subject content. Each exam question is also a review of the concept, making sure that you will get the answer correct without having to go to other sources of material. You learn as you go! Its the easiest way to pass an exam.

HUMOR

Studying can be tedious and dry. MznLnx's instructional design includes moderate humor within the exam questions on occassion, to break the tedium and revitalize the brain

Chapter 1. Prerequisites: Fundamental Concepts of Alaebra 1

1. In algebra, a _____ is a function depending on n that associates a scalar, det(A), to an n×n square matrix A. The fundamental geometric meaning of a _____ is a scale factor for measure when A is regarded as a linear transformation. Determinants are important both in calculus, where they enter the substitution rule for several variables, and in multilinear algebra.

For a fixed nonnegative integer n, there is a unique _____ function for the n×n matrices over any commutative ring R. In particular, this function exists when R is the field of real or complex numbers.

    a. Leibniz formula
    b. Determinant
    c. Functional determinant
    d. Pfaffian

2. In mathematics, the _____ of a real number is its numerical value without regard to its sign. So, for example, 3 is the _____ of both 3 and −3.

The _____ of a number a is denoted by $|a|$.

    a. ADE classification
    b. Abelian P-root group
    c. AKS primality test
    d. Absolute value

3. In mathematics, the complex numbers are an extension of the real numbers obtained by adjoining an imaginary unit, denoted i, which satisfies:

$$i^2 = -1.$$

Every _____ can be written in the form a + bi, where a and b are real numbers called the real part and the imaginary part of the _____, respectively.

Complex numbers are a field, and thus have addition, subtraction, multiplication, and division operations. These operations extend the corresponding operations on real numbers, although with a number of additional elegant and useful properties, e.g., negative real numbers can be obtained by squaring complex (imaginary) numbers.

    a. -equivalence
    b. 2-bridge knot
    c. Complex number
    d. -module

Chapter 1. Prerequisites: Fundamental Concepts of Alaebra

4. In mathematics, the word _____ is a term for any well-formed combination of mathematical symbols. For example,

   $x^2 + 3x - 4$

is an _____, while

)x) / 0

is not, because the parentheses are not balanced and division by zero is undefined.

Being an _____ is a syntactic concept - the meaning of the variables is irrelevant, but different fields have different notions of validity.â€¢See formal language for how expressions are constructed, and formal semantics for meaning.

   a. Arity
   b. Unit ring
   c. Orthogonal
   d. Expression

5. In mathematics, a _____ is a rectangular array of numbers. This way, matrices can record data that depend on multiple parameters. In particular they are used to keep track of the coefficients of multiple linear equations. Matrices are closely connected to linear transformations, which are higher-dimensional analogs of linear functions, i.e., functions of the form f(x) = c Â· x, where c is a constant. This map corresponds to a _____ with one row and column, with entry c. In addition to a number of elementary, entrywise operations such as _____ addition a key notion is _____ multiplication, which displays a number of features not encountered in numbers; for example, products of matrices depend on the order of the factors, unlike products of real numbers, say, where c Â· d = d Â· c for any two numbers c and d.
   a. Commutativity
   b. Polynomial expression
   c. Matrix
   d. Heap

6. In linear algebra, the _____ of a matrix is obtained by changing a matrix in some way.

Given the matrices A and B, where:

$$A = \begin{bmatrix} 1 & 3 & 2 \\ 2 & 0 & 1 \\ 5 & 2 & 2 \end{bmatrix}, \quad B = \begin{bmatrix} 4 \\ 3 \\ 1 \end{bmatrix}$$

Then, the _____ is written as:

$$(A|B) = \begin{bmatrix} 1 & 3 & 2 & 4 \\ 2 & 0 & 1 & 3 \\ 5 & 2 & 2 & 1 \end{bmatrix}$$

This is useful when solving systems of linear equations or the _____ may also be used to find the inverse of a matrix by combining it with the identity matrix.

Let C be a square 2×2 matrix where $C = \begin{bmatrix} 1 & 3 \\ -5 & 0 \end{bmatrix}$

To find the inverse of C we create (C | I) where I is the 2×2 identity matrix.

a. Augmented matrix
b. Euclidean distance matrix
c. Unistochastic matrix
d. Unitary matrix

7. Let S be a set with a binary operation * . If e is an identity element of (S, *) and a * b = e, then a is called a _____ of b and b is called a right inverse of a. If an element x is both a _____ and a right inverse of y, then x is called a two-sided inverse, or simply an inverse, of y.
   a. -module
   b. 2-bridge knot
   c. -equivalence
   d. Left inverse

8. In geometry, a _____ is a straight curve. When geometry is used to model the real world, lines are used to represent straight objects with negligible width and height. Lines are an idealisation of such objects and have no width or height at all and are usually considered to be infinitely long.
   a. 2-bridge knot
   b. -equivalence
   c. Line
   d. -module

9. In mathematics, a _____ is a collection of linear equations involving the same set of variables. For example,

$$3x + 2y - z = 1$$
$$2x - 2y + 4z = -2$$
$$-x + \tfrac{1}{2}y - z = 0$$

is a system of three equations in the three variables x, y, z. A solution to a linear system is an assignment of numbers to the variables such that all the equations are simultaneously satisfied.

a. Simultaneous equations
b. -equivalence
c. -module
d. System of linear equations

10. In mathematics, a _____ or reciprocal for a number x, denoted by $\tfrac{1}{x}$ or x^{-1}, is a number which when multiplied by x yields the multiplicative identity, 1. The _____ of x is also called the reciprocal of x. The _____ of a fraction a/b is b/a.

a. -module
b. -equivalence
c. Multiplicative inverse
d. 2-bridge knot

11. In mathematics, an _____ is a statement about the relative size or order of two objects, or about whether they are the same or not

- The notation a < b means that a is less than b.
- The notation a > b means that a is greater than b.
- The notation a ≠ b means that a is not equal to b, but does not say that one is bigger than the other or even that they can be compared in size.

In all these cases, a is not equal to b, hence, '_____'.

These relations are known as strict _____

- The notation a ≤ b means that a is less than or equal to b (or, equivalently, not greater than b);
- The notation a ≥ b means that a is greater than or equal to b (or, equivalently, not smaller than b);

An additional use of the notation is to show that one quantity is much greater than another, normally by several orders of magnitude.

- The notation a ≪ b means that a is much less than b.
- The notation a ≫ b means that a is much greater than b.

If the sense of the _____ is the same for all values of the variables for which its members are defined, then the _____ is called an 'absolute' or 'unconditional' _____. If the sense of an _____ holds only for certain values of the variables involved, but is reversed or destroyed for other values of the variables, it is called a conditional _____.

One can apply the same algebraic operations to inequalities as one would apply for solving equalities. For example, to find x for the _____ 10x > 20 one would divide 20 by 10 to obtain x > 2.

a. AKS primality test
b. Inequality
c. ADE classification
d. Abelian P-root group

12. In mathematics, a _____ of a number x is any number which, when repeatedly multiplied by itself, eventually yields x:

$$r \times r \times \cdots \times r = x.$$

In terms of exponentiation, r is a _____ of x if

$$r^n = x$$

for some positive integer n. For example, 2 is a _____ of 16 since $2^4 = 2 \times 2 \times 2 \times 2 = 16$.

The number n is called the degree of the _____.

a. Root
b. Cubic function
c. Rationalisation
d. Difference of two squares

13. A _____ is a symbol that stands for a value that may vary; the term usually occurs in opposition to constant, which is a symbol for a non-varying value, i.e. completely fixed or fixed in the context of use. The concepts of constants and variables are fundamental to all modern mathematics, science, engineering, and computer programming.

Chapter 1. Prerequisites: Fundamental Concepts of Alaebra

Much of the basic theory for which we use variables today, such as school geometry and algebra, was developed thousands of years ago, but the use of symbolic formulae and variables is only several hundreds of years old.

   a. 2-bridge knot
   b. -equivalence
   c. -module
   d. Variable

14. _____ is the mathematical process of putting things together. The plus sign '+' means that numbers are added together. For example, in the picture on the right, there are 3 + 2 apples--meaning three apples and two other apples--which is the same as five apples, since 3 + 2 = 5.
   a. ADE classification
   b. Addition
   c. Abelian P-root group
   d. AKS primality test

15. In group theory, a branch of mathematics, the term _____ is used in two closely related senses:

   - the _____ of a group is its cardinality, i.e. the number of its elements;
   - the _____, sometimes period, of an element a of a group is the smallest positive integer m such that a^m = e (where e denotes the identity element of the group, and a^m denotes the product of m copies of a.) If no such m exists, we say that a has infinite _____. All elements of finite groups have finite _____.

We denote the _____ of a group G by ord(G) or $|G|$ and the _____ of an element a by ord(a) or $|a|$.

Example. The symmetric group S_3 has the following multiplication table.

This group has six elements, so ord(S_3) = 6.

   a. Index calculus algorithm
   b. Outer automorphism group
   c. Artin group
   d. Order

16. In algebra and computer programming, when a number or expression is both preceded and followed by an operator such as minus or times, a rule is needed to specify which operator should be applied first; this rule is known as a _____, or more informally order of operation. From the earliest use of mathematical notation, multiplication took precedence over addition, whichever side of a number it appeared on. Thus 3 + 4 × 5 = 5 × 4 + 3 = 23.
   a. Precedence rule
   b. Formal power series
   c. Planar ternary ring
   d. Setoid

17. In its simplest meaning in mathematics and logic, an _____ is an action or procedure which produces a new value from one or more input values. There are two common types of operations: unary and binary. Unary operations involve only one value, such as negation and trigonometric functions.
   a. ADE classification
   b. AKS primality test
   c. Operation
   d. Abelian P-root group

18. In mathematics, the _____ of a number n is the number that, when added to n, yields zero. The _____ of F is denoted −F.

   For example, the _____ of 7 is −7, because 7 + (−7) = 0, and the _____ of −0.3 is 0.3, because −0.3 + 0.3 = 0.

   a. Additive inverse
   b. Artinian ideal
   c. Isomorphism class
   d. Interior algebra

19. In mathematics, the _____ of a polynomial is the term of degree 0. For example, in the polynomial

   $X^3 + 2X + 3$

   over the variable X, the _____ is 3. Here, the _____ is given by a numeral, but it may also be specified by a letter that is a parameter rather than a variable, as in the polynomial

   $ax^2 + bx + c,$

   in the variable x, where a, b, and c are parameters so that c is the _____.

a. Symmetric polynomial
b. Quadratic function
c. Characteristic polynomial
d. Constant term

20. In mathematics, especially in elementary arithmetic, _____ is an arithmetic operation which is the inverse of multiplication.

Specifically, if c times b equals a, written:

$$c \times b = a$$

where b is not zero, then a divided by b equals c, written:

$$\frac{a}{b} = c$$

For instance,

$$\frac{6}{3} = 2$$

since

$$2 \times 3 = 6.$$

In the above expression, a is called the dividend, b the divisor and c the quotient.

a. -module
b. 2-bridge knot
c. Division
d. -equivalence

21. _____ is one of the four basic arithmetic operations; it is the inverse of addition, meaning that if we start with any number and add any number and then subtract the same number we added, we return to the number we started with. _____ is denoted by a minus sign in infix notation.

The traditional names for the parts of the formula

c − b = a

are minuend (c) − subtrahend (b) = difference (a.)

a. Subtraction
b. -equivalence
c. 2-bridge knot
d. -module

22. In mathematics, a _____ is a constant multiplicative factor of a certain object. For example, in the expression 9x², the _____ of x² is 9.

The object can be such things as a variable, a vector, a function, etc.

a. Constant term
b. Coefficient
c. Tschirnhaus transformation
d. Vandermonde polynomial

23. In mathematics, the (formal) _____ of a complex vector space V is the complex vector space $\overline{V}$ consisting of all formal complex conjugates of elements of V. That is, $\overline{V}$ is a vector space whose elements are in one-to-one correspondence with the elements of V:

$$\overline{V} = \{\overline{v} \mid v \in V\},$$

with the following rules for addition and scalar multiplication:

$$\overline{v} + \overline{w} = \overline{v + w} \quad \text{and} \quad \alpha \overline{v} = \overline{\overline{\alpha} v}.$$

Here v and w are vectors in V, α is a complex number, and $\overline{\alpha}$ denotes the _____ of α.

In the case where V is a linear subspace of $\mathbb{C}^n$, the formal _____ $\overline{V}$ is naturally isomorphic to the actual _____ subspace of V in $\mathbb{C}^n$.

a. Polynomial basis
b. Conjugate transpose
c. Binomial inverse theorem
d. Complex conjugate

Chapter 1. Prerequisites: Fundamental Concepts of Alaebra

24. In algebra, a _____ of an element in a quadratic extension field of a field K is its image under the unique non-identity automorphism of the extended field that fixes K. If the extension is generated by a square root of an element r of K, then the _____ of $a + b\sqrt{r}$ is $a - b\sqrt{r}$ for $a, b \in K$, and in particular in the case of the field C of complex numbers as an extension of the field R of real numbers (where r = − 1), the complex _____ of a + bi is a − bi.

Forming the sum or product of any element of the extension field with its _____ always gives an element of K. This can be used to rewrite a quotient of numbers in the extended field so that the denominator lies in K, by multiplying numerator and denominator by the _____ of the denominator. This process is called rationalization of the denominator, in particular if K is the field Q of rational numbers.

a. Field arithmetic
b. Conjugate
c. Digital root
d. K-theory

25. In elementary algebra, a _____ is a polynomial with two terms--the sum of two monomials--often bound by parenthesis or brackets when operated upon. It is the simplest kind of polynomial other than monomials.

- The _____ $a^2 - b^2$ can be factored as the product of two other binomials:

    $a^2 - b^2 = (a + b)(a - b.)$

    This is a special case of the more general formula:

    $$a^{n+1} - b^{n+1} = (a - b) \sum_{k=0}^{n} a^k b^{n-k}$$

- The product of a pair of linear binomials (ax + b) and (cx + d) is:

    $(ax + b)(cx + d) = acx^2 + axd + bcx + bd.$

- A _____ raised to the nth power, represented as

    $(a + b)^n$

    can be expanded by means of the _____ theorem or, equivalently, using Pascal's triangle. Taking a simple example, the perfect square _____ $(p + q)^2$ can be found by squaring the :first digit, adding twice the product of the first and second digit and finally adding the square of the second digit, to give $p^2 + 2pq + q^2$.

a. Theory of equations
b. Binomial
c. Content
d. Generalized arithmetic progression

Chapter 1. Prerequisites: Fundamental Concepts of Alaebra 11

26. In mathematics, the _____ is an important formula giving the expansion of powers of sums. Its simplest version states that

$$(x+y)^n = \sum_{k=0}^{n} \binom{n}{k} x^{n-k} y^k \qquad (1)$$

for any real or complex numbers x and y, and any non-negative integer n. The binomial coefficient appearing in (1) may be defined in terms of the factorial function n!:

$$\binom{n}{k} = \frac{n!}{k!\,(n-k)!}.$$

For example, here are the cases where 2 ≤ n ≤ 5:

$$(x+y)^2 = x^2 + 2xy + y^2$$
$$(x+y)^3 = x^3 + 3x^2y + 3xy^2 + y^3$$
$$(x+y)^4 = x^4 + 4x^3y + 6x^2y^2 + 4xy^3 + y^4$$
$$(x+y)^5 = x^5 + 5x^4y + 10x^3y^2 + 10x^2y^3 + 5xy^4 + y^5.$$

Formula (1) is valid more generally for any elements x and y of a semiring as long as xy = yx.

a. Binomial Theorem
b. -equivalence
c. 2-bridge knot
d. -module

27. The _____ are natural numbers including 0 ' href='/wiki/0_(number)'>0, 1, 2, 3, ...) and their negatives (0, −1, −2, −3, ...). They are numbers that can be written without a fractional or decimal component, and fall within the set {...
a. AKS primality test
b. Integers
c. Abelian P-root group
d. ADE classification

28. The _____ of a Lie algebra $\mathfrak{g}$ is a particular ideal of $\mathfrak{g}$.

Let $\mathfrak{g}$ be a Lie algebra. The _____ of $\mathfrak{g}$ is defined as the largest solvable ideal of $\mathfrak{g}$.

a. Radical
b. Garside element
c. Cyclically reduced word
d. Class sum

29. In mathematics, a _____ of a number x is a number r such that r^2 = x, or, in other words, a number r whose square (the result of multiplying the number by itself) is x.

Every non-negative real number x has a unique non-negative _____, called the principal _____, which is denoted with a radical symbol as $\sqrt{x}$, or, using exponent notation, as $x^{1/2}$. For example, the principal _____ of 9 is 3, denoted $\sqrt{9} = 3$, because 3^2 = 3 × 3 = 9.

a. 2-bridge knot
b. -module
c. Square root
d. -equivalence

30. In mathematics, specifically group theory, the _____ of a subgroup H in a group G is the ¡relative size¿ of H in G. For example, if H has _____ 2 in G, then intuitively ¡half¿ of the elements of G lie in H. The _____ of H in G is usually denoted $|G:H|$ or $[G:H]$.

If G and H are finite groups, then the _____ of H in G is simply the quotient of the orders of the two groups:

$$|G:H| = \frac{|G|}{|H|}.$$

By Lagrange's theorem, this number is always a positive integer.

If G and H are infinite, then the _____ of H is G is defined as the number of cosets of H in G.

a. Inner automorphism
b. Index
c. Even permutations
d. Outer automorphism

31. A _____ is a three-dimensional solid object bounded by six square faces, facets or sides, with three meeting at each vertex. The _____ can also be called a regular hexahedron and is one of the five Platonic solids. It is a special kind of square prism, of rectangular parallelepiped and of trigonal trapezohedron.

a. -module
b. 2-bridge knot
c. -equivalence
d. Cube

32. In mathematics, a _____ of a number, denoted $\sqrt[3]{x}$ or $x^{1/3}$, is a number a such that $a^3 = x$. All real numbers have exactly one real _____ and a pair of complex conjugate roots, and all nonzero complex numbers have three distinct complex cube roots. For example, the real _____ of 8 is 2, because $2^3 = 8$.
   a. 2-bridge knot
   b. -equivalence
   c. -module
   d. Cube root

33. In mathematics, there are several meanings of _____ depending on the subject.

A _____, usually denoted by ° (the _____ symbol), is a measurement of plane angle, representing $1/360$ of a full rotation. When that angle is with respect to a reference meridian, it indicates a location along a great circle of a sphere, such as Earth, Mars, or the celestial sphere.

   a. Symmetric difference
   b. Degree
   c. Median algebra
   d. Relation algebra

34. In mathematics, the word _____ means two different things in the context of polynomials:

   - The first meaning is a product of powers of variables, or formally any value obtained from 1 by finitely many multiplications by a variable. If only a single variable x is considered this means that any _____ is either 1 or a power x^n of x, with n a positive integer. If several variables are considered, say, x, y, z, then each can be given an exponent, so that any _____ is of the form $x^a y^b z^c$ with a,b,c nonnegative integers (taking note that any exponent 0 makes the corresponding factor equal to 1.)
   - The second meaning of _____ includes monomials in the first sense, but also allows multiplication by any constant, so that − $7x^5$ and $(3 − 4i)x^4 yz^{13}$ are also considered to be monomials (the second example assuming polynomials in x, y, z over the complex numbers are considered.)

With either definition, the set of monomials is a subset of all polynomials that is closed under multiplication.

Chapter 1. Prerequisites: Fundamental Concepts of Alaebra

Both uses of this notion can be found, and in many cases the distinction is simply ignored, see for instance examples for the first and second meaning, and an unclear definition. In informal discussions the distinction is seldom important, and tendency is towards the broader second meaning. When studying the structure of polynomials however, one often definitely needs a notion with the first meaning.

   a. Diagonal form
   b. Schur polynomials
   c. Power sum symmetric polynomial
   d. Monomial

35. In elementary algebra, a _____ is a polynomial consisting of three terms; in other words, a _____ is the sum of three monomials. It can be factored using simple steps.

In linguistics, a _____ is a fixed expression which is made from three words; e.g. 'lights, camera, action', 'signed, sealed, delivered'.

   a. Trinomial
   b. Hall polynomials
   c. Polynomial Diophantine equation
   d. Finitary operation

36. In mathematics, the adjective _____ means that an object cannot be expressed as a product of more than one non-trivial factors in a given set. See also factorization.

For any field F, the ring of polynomials with coefficients in F is denoted by F[x].

   a. Alternating polynomial
   b. Integer-valued polynomial
   c. Ehrhart polynomial
   d. Irreducible

37. In mathematics, _____(F_n) is the outer automorphism group of a free group on n generators. These groups play an important role in geometric group theory.

_____(F_n) acts geometrically on a cell complex known as outer space, which can be thought of as the Teichmüller space for a bouquet of circles.

a. AKS primality test
b. ADE classification
c. Out
d. Abelian P-root group

38. In mathematics, the _____ is when a number is squared and is then subtracted from another squared number. It refers to the identity

$$a^2 - b^2 = (a+b)(a-b)$$

from elementary algebra.

The proof is straightforward, starting from the RHS: apply the distributive law to get a sum of four terms, and set

$$ba - ab = 0$$

as an application of the commutative law.

a. Pointwise product
b. FOIL rule
c. Cubic function
d. Difference of two squares

39. In mathematics, _____ or factoring is the decomposition of an object ' href='/wiki/Matrix_(mathematics)'>matrix) into a product of other objects, or factors, which when multiplied together give the original. For example, the number 15 factors into primes as 3 × 5, and the polynomial $x^2 - 4$ factors as (x − 2)(x + 2.) In all cases, a product of simpler objects is obtained.
a. 2-bridge knot
b. -module
c. Factorization
d. -equivalence

40. In mathematics, especially in the area of abstract algebra known as ring theory, a _____ is a ring with 0 ≠ 1 such that ab = 0 implies that either a = 0 or b = 0 (the zero-product property.) That is, it is a nontrivial ring without left or right zero divisors. A commutative _____ is called an integral _____.

a. Coherent ring
b. Partially-ordered ring
c. Subring
d. Domain

Chapter 2. Equations, Inequalities, and Mathematical Models

1. _____, usually called coordinate geometry and earlier referred to as Cartesian geometry or analytical geometry, is the study of geometry using the principles of algebra; the modern development of _____ is thus suggestively called algebraic geometry.

Usually the Cartesian coordinate system is applied to manipulate equations for planes, straight lines, and squares, often in two and sometimes in three dimensions of measurement. Geometrical, one studies the Euclidean plane (2 dimensions) and Euclidean space (3 dimensions.)

   a. Enumerative geometry
   b. Analytic geometry
   c. ADE classification
   d. AKS primality test

2. In mathematics, the _____ of a real number is its numerical value without regard to its sign. So, for example, 3 is the _____ of both 3 and −3.

The _____ of a number a is denoted by $|a|$.

   a. Abelian P-root group
   b. ADE classification
   c. AKS primality test
   d. Absolute value

3. In mathematics, a (B, N) _____ is a structure on groups of Lie type that allows one to give uniform proofs of many results, instead of giving a large number of case-by-case proofs. Roughly speaking, it shows that all such groups are similar to the general linear group over a field. They were invented by the mathematician Jacques Tits, and are also sometimes known as Tits systems.
   a. Rank of a group
   b. Pair
   c. Group action
   d. Group representations

4. In mathematics, a _____ is a polynomial equation of the second degree. The general form is

$$ax^2 + bx + c = 0$$

The quadratic coefficient a is the coefficient of x^2, the linear coefficient b is the coefficient of x, and c is the constant coefficient, also called the free term or constant term.

Quadratic equations are called quadratic because the variable in the leading term is squared.

Chapter 2. Equations, Inequalities, and Mathematical Models

   a. Quadratic equation
   b. Rationalisation
   c. Difference of two squares
   d. Cubic function

5. In group theory, a branch of mathematics, the term _____ is used in two closely related senses:

   - the _____ of a group is its cardinality, i.e. the number of its elements;
   - the _____, sometimes period, of an element a of a group is the smallest positive integer m such that a^m = e (where e denotes the identity element of the group, and a^m denotes the product of m copies of a.) If no such m exists, we say that a has infinite _____. All elements of finite groups have finite _____.

We denote the _____ of a group G by ord(G) or $|G|$ and the _____ of an element a by ord(a) or $|a|$.

Example. The symmetric group S_3 has the following multiplication table.

This group has six elements, so ord(S_3) = 6.

   a. Outer automorphism group
   b. Order
   c. Artin group
   d. Index calculus algorithm

6. A _____ is a symbol that stands for a value that may vary; the term usually occurs in opposition to constant, which is a symbol for a non-varying value, i.e. completely fixed or fixed in the context of use. The concepts of constants and variables are fundamental to all modern mathematics, science, engineering, and computer programming.

Much of the basic theory for which we use variables today, such as school geometry and algebra, was developed thousands of years ago, but the use of symbolic formulae and variables is only several hundreds of years old.

   a. 2-bridge knot
   b. -equivalence
   c. -module
   d. Variable

7. In geometry, a _____ is a straight curve. When geometry is used to model the real world, lines are used to represent straight objects with negligible width and height. Lines are an idealisation of such objects and have no width or height at all and are usually considered to be infinitely long.

a. -equivalence
b. Line
c. 2-bridge knot
d. -module

8. In mathematics, a _____ of a number x is any number which, when repeatedly multiplied by itself, eventually yields x:

$$r \times r \times \cdots \times r = x.$$

In terms of exponentiation, r is a _____ of x if

$$r^n = x$$

for some positive integer n. For example, 2 is a _____ of 16 since $2^4 = 2 \times 2 \times 2 \times 2 = 16$.

The number n is called the degree of the _____.

a. Rationalisation
b. Difference of two squares
c. Cubic function
d. Root

9. In mathematics, the word _____ is a term for any well-formed combination of mathematical symbols. For example,

$$x^2 + 3x - 4$$

is an _____, while

)x) / 0

is not, because the parentheses are not balanced and division by zero is undefined.

Being an _____ is a syntactic concept - the meaning of the variables is irrelevant, but different fields have different notions of validity.âSee formal language for how expressions are constructed, and formal semantics for meaning.

a. Unit ring
b. Arity
c. Expression
d. Orthogonal

10. In mathematics, and more specifically set theory, the _____ is the unique set having no (zero) members. Some axiomatic set theories assure that the _____ exists by including an axiom of _____; in other theories, its existence can be deduced. Many possible properties of sets are trivially true for the _____.

a. Abelian P-root group
b. ADE classification
c. AKS primality test
d. Empty set

11. In elementary algebra, a _____ is a polynomial with two terms--the sum of two monomials--often bound by parenthesis or brackets when operated upon. It is the simplest kind of polynomial other than monomials.

- The _____ $a^2 - b^2$ can be factored as the product of two other binomials:

    $a^2 - b^2 = (a + b)(a - b.)$

    This is a special case of the more general formula:

    $$a^{n+1} - b^{n+1} = (a - b) \sum_{k=0}^{n} a^k b^{n-k}$$

- The product of a pair of linear binomials (ax + b) and (cx + d) is:

    $(ax + b)(cx + d) = acx^2 + axd + bcx + bd.$

- A _____ raised to the nth power, represented as

    $(a + b)^n$

    can be expanded by means of the _____ theorem or, equivalently, using Pascal's triangle. Taking a simple example, the perfect square _____ $(p + q)^2$ can be found by squaring the :first digit, adding twice the product of the first and second digit and finally adding the square of the second digit, to give $p^2 + 2pq + q^2$.

a. Content
b. Theory of equations
c. Generalized arithmetic progression
d. Binomial

12. In mathematics, the _____ is an important formula giving the expansion of powers of sums. Its simplest version states that

$$(x+y)^n = \sum_{k=0}^{n} \binom{n}{k} x^{n-k} y^k \qquad (1)$$

for any real or complex numbers x and y, and any non-negative integer n. The binomial coefficient appearing in (1) may be defined in terms of the factorial function n!:

$$\binom{n}{k} = \frac{n!}{k!(n-k)!}.$$

For example, here are the cases where 2 ≤ n ≤ 5:

$$(x+y)^2 = x^2 + 2xy + y^2$$
$$(x+y)^3 = x^3 + 3x^2y + 3xy^2 + y^3$$
$$(x+y)^4 = x^4 + 4x^3y + 6x^2y^2 + 4xy^3 + y^4$$
$$(x+y)^5 = x^5 + 5x^4y + 10x^3y^2 + 10x^2y^3 + 5xy^4 + y^5.$$

Formula (1) is valid more generally for any elements x and y of a semiring as long as xy = yx.

a. 2-bridge knot
b. -module
c. Binomial Theorem
d. -equivalence

13. In mathematics, the term _____ is used to describe an algebraic structures which in some sense cannot be divided by a smaller structure of the same type. Put another way, an algebraic structure is _____ if the kernel of every homomorphism is either the whole structure or a single element. Some examples are:

- A group is called a _____ group if it does not contain a non-trivial proper normal subgroup.
- A ring is called a _____ ring if it does not contain a non-trivial two sided ideal.
- A module is called a _____ module if does not contain a non-trivial submodule.
- An algebra is called a _____ algebra if does not contain a non-trivial two sided ideal.

The general pattern is that the structure admits no non-trivial congruence relations.

a. Polarization identity
b. Commutativity
c. Simple
d. Linear combinations

14. In mathematics, the complex numbers are an extension of the real numbers obtained by adjoining an imaginary unit, denoted i, which satisfies:

$$i^2 = -1.$$

Every _____ can be written in the form a + bi, where a and b are real numbers called the real part and the imaginary part of the _____, respectively.

Complex numbers are a field, and thus have addition, subtraction, multiplication, and division operations. These operations extend the corresponding operations on real numbers, although with a number of additional elegant and useful properties, e.g., negative real numbers can be obtained by squaring complex (imaginary) numbers.

a. Complex number
b. -equivalence
c. 2-bridge knot
d. -module

15. In mathematics, a _____ of a number x is a number r such that r^2 = x, or, in other words, a number r whose square (the result of multiplying the number by itself) is x.

Every non-negative real number x has a unique non-negative _____, called the principal _____, which is denoted with a radical symbol as $\sqrt{x}$, or, using exponent notation, as $x^{1/2}$. For example, the principal _____ of 9 is 3, denoted $\sqrt{9} = 3$, because 3^2 = 3 × 3 = 9.

a. -equivalence
b. -module
c. 2-bridge knot
d. Square root

16. In mathematics, a _____ in a (unital) ring R is an invertible element of R, i.e. an element u such that there is a v in R with

$uv = vu = 1_R$, where 1_R is the multiplicative identity element.

That is, u is an invertible element of the multiplicative monoid of R. If $0 \neq 1$ in the ring, then 0 is not a _____.

Unfortunately, the term _____ is also used to refer to the identity element 1_R of the ring, in expressions like ring with a _____ or _____ ring, and also e.g. '_____' matrix.

a. Unit
b. Ore condition
c. Ore extension
d. Ascending chain condition on principal ideals

17. _____ is the mathematical process of putting things together. The plus sign '+' means that numbers are added together. For example, in the picture on the right, there are 3 + 2 apples--meaning three apples and two other apples--which is the same as five apples, since 3 + 2 = 5.
a. AKS primality test
b. Abelian P-root group
c. Addition
d. ADE classification

18. _____ is one of the four basic arithmetic operations; it is the inverse of addition, meaning that if we start with any number and add any number and then subtract the same number we added, we return to the number we started with. _____ is denoted by a minus sign in infix notation.

The traditional names for the parts of the formula

    c − b = a

are minuend (c) − subtrahend (b) = difference (a.)

a. Subtraction
b. -equivalence
c. 2-bridge knot
d. -module

Chapter 2. Equations, Inequalities, and Mathematical Models

19. In its simplest meaning in mathematics and logic, an _____ is an action or procedure which produces a new value from one or more input values. There are two common types of operations: unary and binary. Unary operations involve only one value, such as negation and trigonometric functions.
   a. AKS primality test
   b. ADE classification
   c. Abelian P-root group
   d. Operation

20. In mathematics, the (formal) _____ of a complex vector space V is the complex vector space $\overline{V}$ consisting of all formal complex conjugates of elements of V. That is, $\overline{V}$ is a vector space whose elements are in one-to-one correspondence with the elements of V:

$$\overline{V} = \{\overline{v} \mid v \in V\},$$

with the following rules for addition and scalar multiplication:

$$\overline{v} + \overline{w} = \overline{v + w} \quad \text{and} \quad \alpha \overline{v} = \overline{\overline{\alpha} v}.$$

Here v and w are vectors in V, α is a complex number, and $\overline{\alpha}$ denotes the _____ of α.

In the case where V is a linear subspace of $\mathbb{C}^n$, the formal _____ $\overline{V}$ is naturally isomorphic to the actual _____ subspace of V in $\mathbb{C}^n$.

   a. Polynomial basis
   b. Conjugate transpose
   c. Binomial inverse theorem
   d. Complex conjugate

21. In mathematics, especially in elementary arithmetic, _____ is an arithmetic operation which is the inverse of multiplication.

Specifically, if c times b equals a, written:

$$c \times b = a$$

where b is not zero, then a divided by b equals c, written:

$$\frac{a}{b} = c$$

For instance,

$$\frac{6}{3} = 2$$

since

$$2 \times 3 = 6.$$

In the above expression, a is called the dividend, b the divisor and c the quotient.

a. 2-bridge knot
b. Division
c. -equivalence
d. -module

22. In algebra, a _____ of an element in a quadratic extension field of a field K is its image under the unique non-identity automorphism of the extended field that fixes K. If the extension is generated by a square root of an element r of K, then the _____ of $a + b\sqrt{r}$ is $a - b\sqrt{r}$ for $a, b \in K$, and in particular in the case of the field C of complex numbers as an extension of the field R of real numbers (where r = − 1), the complex _____ of a + bi is a − bi.

Forming the sum or product of any element of the extension field with its _____ always gives an element of K. This can be used to rewrite a quotient of numbers in the extended field so that the denominator lies in K, by multiplying numerator and denominator by the _____ of the denominator. This process is called rationalization of the denominator, in particular if K is the field Q of rational numbers.

a. Field arithmetic
b. Digital root
c. K-theory
d. Conjugate

23. In elementary algebra, _____ is a technique for converting a quadratic polynomial of the form

$$ax^2 + bx + c$$

to the form

$$a(\cdots\cdots)^2 + \text{constant}.$$

The expression inside the parenthesis is of the form x − constant. Thus one converts ax² + bx + c to

$$a(x - h)^2 + k$$

and one must find h and k.

_____ is used in

- solving quadratic equations,
- graphing quadratic functions,
- evaluating integrals in calculus,
- finding Laplace transforms.

In mathematics, _____ is considered a basic algebraic operation, and is often applied without remark in any computation involving quadratic polynomials.

There is a simple formula in elementary algebra for computing the square of a binomial:

$$(x + p)^2 = x^2 + 2px + p^2.$$

For example:

$$(x + 3)^2 = x^2 + 6x + 9 \qquad (p = 3)$$
$$(x - 5)^2 = x^2 - 10x + 25 \qquad (p = -5).$$

In any perfect square, the number p is always half the coefficient of x, and then the constant term is equal to p².

a. Nested radical
b. Content
c. Completing the square
d. Reduct

24. In elementary algebra, a _____ is a polynomial consisting of three terms; in other words, a _____ is the sum of three monomials. It can be factored using simple steps.

In linguistics, a _____ is a fixed expression which is made from three words; e.g. 'lights, camera, action', 'signed, sealed, delivered'.

a. Polynomial Diophantine equation
b. Hall polynomials
c. Trinomial
d. Finitary operation

25. In algebra, the _____ of a polynomial with real or complex coefficients is a certain expression in the coefficients of the polynomial which is a symmetric polynomial in the coefficients and gives information on the nature of the roots; in particular, it is equal to zero if and only if the polynomial has a multiple root (i.e. a root with multiplicity greater than one) in the complex numbers. For example, the _____ of the quadratic polynomial

$ax^2 + bx + c$ is $b^2 - 4ac$.

The _____ of the cubic polynomial

$ax^3 + bx^2 + cx + d$ is $b^2c^2 - 4ac^3 - 4b^3d - 27a^2d^2 + 18abcd$.

a. Polynomial remainder theorem
b. Minimal polynomial
c. Kazhdan-Lusztig polynomials
d. Discriminant

26. A _____ is a triangle in which one angle is a right angle.

The side opposite the right angle is called the hypotenuse (side [BC] in the figure below.) In addition, the sides adjacent to the right angle are called legs or catheti (singular: cathetus.)

a. -equivalence
b. 2-bridge knot
c. Right triangle
d. -module

27. A _____ is one of the basic shapes of geometry: a polygon with three corners or vertices and three sides or edges which are line segments. A _____ with vertices A, B, and C is denoted ABC.

In Euclidean geometry any three non-collinear points determine a unique _____ and a unique plane (i.e. a two-dimensional Euclidean space.)

Chapter 2. Equations, Inequalities, and Mathematical Models

   a. 2-bridge knot
   b. Triangle
   c. -equivalence
   d. -module

28. The _____ of a Lie algebra $\mathfrak{g}$ is a particular ideal of $\mathfrak{g}$.

Let $\mathfrak{g}$ be a Lie algebra. The _____ of $\mathfrak{g}$ is defined as the largest solvable ideal of $\mathfrak{g}$.

   a. Garside element
   b. Class sum
   c. Cyclically reduced word
   d. Radical

29. In mathematics, an _____ represents a solution, such as that to an equation, that emerges from the process of solving the problem but is not a valid solution to the original problem. A missing solution is a solution that was a valid solution to the original problem, but disappeared during the process of solving the problem. Both are frequently the consequence of performing operations that are not invertible for some or all values of the variables, which disturbs the chain of logical implications in the proof.
   a. Unary operation
   b. Unitary method
   c. Equating the coefficients
   d. Extraneous solution

30. In mathematics, an _____ is a statement about the relative size or order of two objects, or about whether they are the same or not

   - The notation a < b means that a is less than b.
   - The notation a > b means that a is greater than b.
   - The notation a ≠ b means that a is not equal to b, but does not say that one is bigger than the other or even that they can be compared in size.

In all these cases, a is not equal to b, hence, '_____'.

These relations are known as strict _____

   - The notation a ≤ b means that a is less than or equal to b (or, equivalently, not greater than b);
   - The notation a ≥ b means that a is greater than or equal to b (or, equivalently, not smaller than b);

Chapter 2. Equations, Inequalities, and Mathematical Models

An additional use of the notation is to show that one quantity is much greater than another, normally by several orders of magnitude.

- The notation a ≪ b means that a is much less than b.
- The notation a ≫ b means that a is much greater than b.

If the sense of the _____ is the same for all values of the variables for which its members are defined, then the _____ is called an 'absolute' or 'unconditional' _____. If the sense of an _____ holds only for certain values of the variables involved, but is reversed or destroyed for other values of the variables, it is called a conditional _____.

One can apply the same algebraic operations to inequalities as one would apply for solving equalities. For example, to find x for the _____ 10x > 20 one would divide 20 by 10 to obtain x > 2.

a. AKS primality test
b. Inequality
c. ADE classification
d. Abelian P-root group

Chapter 3. Functions and Graphs

1. In geometry, two lines or planes (or a line and a plane), are considered _____ to each other if they form congruent adjacent angles (an L-shape.) The term may be used as a noun or adjective. Thus, referring to Figure 1, the line AB is the _____ to CD through the point B. Note that by definition, a line is infinitely long, and strictly speaking AB and CD in this example represent line segments of two infinitely long lines.
    a. -equivalence
    b. -module
    c. 2-bridge knot
    d. Perpendicular

2. In geometry, a _____ is a straight curve. When geometry is used to model the real world, lines are used to represent straight objects with negligible width and height. Lines are an idealisation of such objects and have no width or height at all and are usually considered to be infinitely long.
    a. -equivalence
    b. 2-bridge knot
    c. Line
    d. -module

3. In elementary algebra, a _____ is a polynomial with two terms--the sum of two monomials--often bound by parenthesis or brackets when operated upon. It is the simplest kind of polynomial other than monomials.

    - The _____ $a^2 - b^2$ can be factored as the product of two other binomials:

        $a^2 - b^2 = (a + b)(a - b.)$

        This is a special case of the more general formula: $a^{n+1} - b^{n+1} = (a - b) \sum_{k=0}^{n} a^k b^{n-k}$.

    - The product of a pair of linear binomials (ax + b) and (cx + d) is:

        $(ax + b)(cx + d) = acx^2 + axd + bcx + bd.$

    - A _____ raised to the nth power, represented as

        $(a + b)^n$

        can be expanded by means of the _____ theorem or, equivalently, using Pascal's triangle. Taking a simple example, the perfect square _____ $(p + q)^2$ can be found by squaring the :first digit, adding twice the product of the first and second digit and finally adding the square of the second digit, to give $p^2 + 2pq + q^2$.

Chapter 3. Functions and Graphs 31

 a. Content
 b. Generalized arithmetic progression
 c. Theory of equations
 d. Binomial

4. In mathematics, the _____ is an important formula giving the expansion of powers of sums. Its simplest version states that

$$(x+y)^n = \sum_{k=0}^{n} \binom{n}{k} x^{n-k} y^k \quad (1)$$

for any real or complex numbers x and y, and any non-negative integer n. The binomial coefficient appearing in (1) may be defined in terms of the factorial function n!:

$$\binom{n}{k} = \frac{n!}{k!\,(n-k)!}.$$

For example, here are the cases where $2 \leq n \leq 5$:

$$(x+y)^2 = x^2 + 2xy + y^2$$
$$(x+y)^3 = x^3 + 3x^2 y + 3xy^2 + y^3$$
$$(x+y)^4 = x^4 + 4x^3 y + 6x^2 y^2 + 4xy^3 + y^4$$
$$(x+y)^5 = x^5 + 5x^4 y + 10x^3 y^2 + 10x^2 y^3 + 5xy^4 + y^5.$$

Formula (1) is valid more generally for any elements x and y of a semiring as long as xy = yx.

 a. -equivalence
 b. 2-bridge knot
 c. -module
 d. Binomial Theorem

5. The term _____ or centre is used in various contexts in abstract algebra to denote the set of all those elements that commute with all other elements. More specifically:

- The _____ of a group G consists of all those elements x in G such that xg = gx for all g in G. This is a normal subgroup of G.
- The _____ of a ring R is the subset of R consisting of all those elements x of R such that xr = rx for all r in R. The _____ is a commutative subring of R, so R is an algebra over its _____.
- The _____ of an algebra A consists of all those elements x of A such that xa = ax for all a in A. See also: central simple algebra.
- The _____ of a Lie algebra L consists of all those elements x in L such that [x,a] = 0 for all a in L. This is an ideal of the Lie algebra L.
- The _____ of a monoidal category C consists of pairs (A,u) where A is an object of C, and $u : A \otimes - \to - \otimes A$ a natural isomorphism satisfying certain axioms.

a. Ring theory
b. Self-adjoint
c. Left alternative
d. Center

6. In mathematics, especially in the area of abstract algebra known as ring theory, a _____ is a ring with 0 ≠ 1 such that ab = 0 implies that either a = 0 or b = 0 (the zero-product property.) That is, it is a nontrivial ring without left or right zero divisors. A commutative _____ is called an integral _____.

a. Coherent ring
b. Domain
c. Partially-ordered ring
d. Subring

7. A _____, in mathematics, is a polynomial function of the form f(x) = ax² + bx + c = 0, where $a \neq 0$. The graph of a _____ is a parabola whose major axis is parallel to the y-axis.

The expression ax² + bx + c in the definition of a _____ is a polynomial of degree 2 or second order, or a 2nd degree polynomial, because the highest exponent of x is 2.

a. Vandermonde polynomial
b. Dickson polynomials
c. Factor theorem
d. Quadratic function

8. In mathematics, a _____ is any function which can be written as the ratio of two polynomial functions. _____ of degree 2 :
$$y = \frac{x^2 - 3x - 2}{x^2 - 4}$$

In the case of one variable, x, a _____ is a function of the form

$$f(x) = \frac{P(x)}{Q(x)}$$

where P and Q are polynomial function in x and Q is not the zero polynomial. The domain of f is the set of all points x for which the denominator Q(x) is not zero.

a. Legendre rational functions
b. Rational function
c. -module
d. -equivalence

9. _____ is the mathematical process of putting things together. The plus sign '+' means that numbers are added together. For example, in the picture on the right, there are 3 + 2 apples--meaning three apples and two other apples--which is the same as five apples, since 3 + 2 = 5.
a. Addition
b. ADE classification
c. Abelian P-root group
d. AKS primality test

10. In mathematics, a _____ is a polynomial equation of the second degree. The general form is

$$ax^2 + bx + c = 0$$

The quadratic coefficient a is the coefficient of x^2, the linear coefficient b is the coefficient of x, and c is the constant coefficient, also called the free term or constant term.

Quadratic equations are called quadratic because the variable in the leading term is squared.

a. Quadratic equation
b. Difference of two squares
c. Rationalisation
d. Cubic function

Chapter 3. Functions and Graphs

11. A _____ is a symbol that stands for a value that may vary; the term usually occurs in opposition to constant, which is a symbol for a non-varying value, i.e. completely fixed or fixed in the context of use. The concepts of constants and variables are fundamental to all modern mathematics, science, engineering, and computer programming.

Much of the basic theory for which we use variables today, such as school geometry and algebra, was developed thousands of years ago, but the use of symbolic formulae and variables is only several hundreds of years old.

   a. 2-bridge knot
   b. -module
   c. Variable
   d. -equivalence

12. An _____ is a pointed projectile that is shot with a bow. It predates recorded history and is common to most cultures. Schematic of an _____ with many parts.

A normal _____ consists of a shaft with an arrowhead attached to the front end, with fletchings and a nock at the other.

   a. ADE classification
   b. AKS primality test
   c. Abelian P-root group
   d. Arrow

13. In a totally ordered set all elements are mutually comparable, so such a set can have at most one minimal element and at most one maximal element. Then, due to mutual comparability, the minimal element will also be the least element and the maximal element will also be the greatest element. Thus in a totally ordered set we can simply use the terms _____ and maximum.
   a. Minimum
   b. -equivalence
   c. 2-bridge knot
   d. -module

14. The set of all symmetry operations considered, on all objects in a set X, can be modeled as a group action g : G × X → X, where the image of g in G and x in X is written as gÂ·x. If, for some g, gÂ·x = y then x and y are said to be symmetrical to each other. For each object x, operations g for which gÂ·x = x form a group, the _____ of the object, a subgroup of G. If the _____ of x is the trivial group then x is said to be asymmetric, otherwise symmetric.

Chapter 3. Functions and Graphs

a. 2-bridge knot
b. -module
c. Symmetry group
d. -equivalence

15. In mathematics, the _____ of a real number is its numerical value without regard to its sign. So, for example, 3 is the _____ of both 3 and −3.

The _____ of a number a is denoted by $|a|$.

a. AKS primality test
b. Abelian P-root group
c. ADE classification
d. Absolute value

16. The _____ are natural numbers including 0 ' href='/wiki/0_(number)'>0, 1, 2, 3, ...) and their negatives (0, −1, −2, −3, ...). They are numbers that can be written without a fractional or decimal component, and fall within the set {...

a. AKS primality test
b. ADE classification
c. Abelian P-root group
d. Integers

17. In mathematics, a _____ is a rectangular array of numbers. This way, matrices can record data that depend on multiple parameters. In particular they are used to keep track of the coefficients of multiple linear equations. Matrices are closely connected to linear transformations, which are higher-dimensional analogs of linear functions, i.e., functions of the form f(x) = c Â· x, where c is a constant. This map corresponds to a _____ with one row and column, with entry c. In addition to a number of elementary, entrywise operations such as _____ addition a key notion is _____ multiplication, which displays a number of features not encountered in numbers; for example, products of matrices depend on the order of the factors, unlike products of real numbers, say, where c Â· d = d Â· c for any two numbers c and d.

a. Heap
b. Polynomial expression
c. Commutativity
d. Matrix

18. In mathematics, a _____ is a function of the form

Chapter 3. Functions and Graphs

$$f(x) = ax^3 + bx^2 + cx + d,$$

where a is nonzero; or in other words, a polynomial of degree three. The derivative of a _____ is a quadratic function. The integral of a _____ is a quartic function.

a. Difference of two squares
b. Rationalisation
c. FOIL rule
d. Cubic function

19. In mathematics, a _____ of a number x is a number r such that $r^2 = x$, or, in other words, a number r whose square (the result of multiplying the number by itself) is x.

Every non-negative real number x has a unique non-negative _____, called the principal _____, which is denoted with a radical symbol as $\sqrt{x}$, or, using exponent notation, as $x^{1/2}$. For example, the principal _____ of 9 is 3, denoted $\sqrt{9} = 3$, because $3^2 = 3 \times 3 = 9$.

a. -module
b. Square root
c. -equivalence
d. 2-bridge knot

20. In mathematics, a _____ of a number x is any number which, when repeatedly multiplied by itself, eventually yields x:

$$r \times r \times \cdots \times r = x.$$

In terms of exponentiation, r is a _____ of x if

$$r^n = x$$

for some positive integer n. For example, 2 is a _____ of 16 since $2^4 = 2 \times 2 \times 2 \times 2 = 16$.

The number n is called the degree of the _____.

a. Root
b. Rationalisation
c. Difference of two squares
d. Cubic function

21. In linear algebra, a _____ is a linear transformation that squares to the identity ($R^2 = I$, where R is in K dimensional space), also known as an involution in the general linear group. In addition to reflections across hyperplanes, the class of general reflections includes point reflections, reflections across subspaces of intermediate dimension, and non-orthogonal reflections.

A _____ over a hyperplane in an inner product space is necessarily symmetric, but a general _____ need not be as the example $\begin{bmatrix} 1 & 0 \\ 1 & -1 \end{bmatrix}$ shows.

a. Morphism
b. Shear mappings
c. Homomorphic secret sharing
d. Reflection

22. In algebra, a commutative ring R is said to be _____ if any of the following equivalent conditions holds:

1. The localization R_m of R at m is a valuation ring for every maximal ideal m of R.
2. For all ideals a, b, and c,

$$a \cap (b + c) = (a \cap b) + (a \cap c)$$

- For all ideals a, b, and c,

$$a + (b \cap c) = (a + b) \cap (a + c)$$

An _____ domain is called a Prüfer domain.

a. Arithmetical
b. Exchange matrix
c. Ordered vector space
d. Inverse eigenvalues theorem

23. In mathematics, a _____ represents the application of one function to the results of another. For instance, the functions f: X → Y and g: Y → Z can be composed by first computing f(x) and then applying a function g to the output of f(x.)

Thus one obtains a function g ∘ f: X → Z defined by (g ∘ f)(x) = g(f(x)) for all x in X. The notation g ∘ f is read as 'g circle f', or 'g composed with f', 'g after f', 'g following f', or just 'g of f'.

a. Linear map
b. Reflection
c. Shear mappings
d. Composite function

Chapter 4. Polynomial and Rational Functions

1. In mathematics, the _____ is a conic section, the intersection of a right circular conical surface and a plane parallel to a generating straight line of that surface. Given a point (the focus) and a line (the directrix) that lie in a plane, the locus of points in that plane that are equidistant to them is a _____.

A particular case arises when the plane is tangent to the conical surface of a circle.

   a. -equivalence
   b. Parabola
   c. 2-bridge knot
   d. -module

2. A _____, in mathematics, is a polynomial function of the form f(x) = ax² + bx + c = 0, where $a \neq 0$. The graph of a _____ is a parabola whose major axis is parallel to the y-axis.

The expression ax² + bx + c in the definition of a _____ is a polynomial of degree 2 or second order, or a 2nd degree polynomial, because the highest exponent of x is 2.

   a. Factor theorem
   b. Vandermonde polynomial
   c. Quadratic function
   d. Dickson polynomials

3. In mathematics, an _____ is the finite or bounded case of a conic section, the geometric shape that results from cutting a circular conical or cylindrical surface with an oblique plane . It is also the locus of all points of the plane whose distances to two fixed points add to the same constant.

Ellipses also arise as images of a circle or a sphere under parallel projection, and some cases of perspective projection.

   a. ADE classification
   b. AKS primality test
   c. Abelian P-root group
   d. Ellipse

4. In elementary algebra, _____ is a technique for converting a quadratic polynomial of the form

$$ax^2 + bx + c$$

to the form

$$a(\cdots\cdots)^2 + \text{constant}.$$

The expression inside the parenthesis is of the form x − constant. Thus one converts ax² + bx + c to

$$a(x - h)^2 + k$$

and one must find h and k.

_____ is used in

- solving quadratic equations,
- graphing quadratic functions,
- evaluating integrals in calculus,
- finding Laplace transforms.

In mathematics, _____ is considered a basic algebraic operation, and is often applied without remark in any computation involving quadratic polynomials.

There is a simple formula in elementary algebra for computing the square of a binomial:

$$(x + p)^2 = x^2 + 2px + p^2.$$

For example:

$$(x + 3)^2 = x^2 + 6x + 9 \qquad (p = 3)$$
$$(x - 5)^2 = x^2 - 10x + 25 \qquad (p = -5).$$

In any perfect square, the number p is always half the coefficient of x, and then the constant term is equal to p².

a. Nested radical
b. Completing the square
c. Reduct
d. Content

Chapter 4. Polynomial and Rational Functions

5. In a totally ordered set all elements are mutually comparable, so such a set can have at most one minimal element and at most one maximal element. Then, due to mutual comparability, the minimal element will also be the least element and the maximal element will also be the greatest element. Thus in a totally ordered set we can simply use the terms _____ and maximum.

   a. 2-bridge knot
   b. -module
   c. -equivalence
   d. Minimum

6. In mathematics, a _____ is a constant multiplicative factor of a certain object. For example, in the expression $9x^2$, the _____ of x^2 is 9.

   The object can be such things as a variable, a vector, a function, etc.

   a. Tschirnhaus transformation
   b. Constant term
   c. Vandermonde polynomial
   d. Coefficient

7. In mathematics, a _____ of a number x is any number which, when repeatedly multiplied by itself, eventually yields x:

   $$r \times r \times \cdots \times r = x.$$

   In terms of exponentiation, r is a _____ of x if

   $$r^n = x$$

   for some positive integer n. For example, 2 is a _____ of 16 since $2^4 = 2 \times 2 \times 2 \times 2 = 16$.

   The number n is called the degree of the _____.

   a. Root
   b. Rationalisation
   c. Cubic function
   d. Difference of two squares

8. In mathematics, there are several meanings of _____ depending on the subject.

A _____, usually denoted by ° (the _____ symbol), is a measurement of plane angle, representing $\frac{1}{360}$ of a full rotation. When that angle is with respect to a reference meridian, it indicates a location along a great circle of a sphere, such as Earth, Mars, or the celestial sphere.

a. Relation algebra
b. Symmetric difference
c. Median algebra
d. Degree

9. In mathematics, especially in elementary arithmetic, _____ is an arithmetic operation which is the inverse of multiplication.

Specifically, if c times b equals a, written:

$$c \times b = a$$

where b is not zero, then a divided by b equals c, written:

$$\frac{a}{b} = c$$

For instance,

$$\frac{6}{3} = 2$$

since

$$2 \times 3 = 6.$$

In the above expression, a is called the dividend, b the divisor and c the quotient.

a. -module
b. 2-bridge knot
c. -equivalence
d. Division

10. In algebra, the _____ is a theorem for finding out the factors of a polynomial (an expression in which the terms are only added, subtracted or multiplied, e.g. $x^2 + 6x + 6$.) It is a special case of the polynomial remainder theorem.

The _____ states that a polynomial f(x) has a factor x − k if and only if f(k) = 0.

a. Quadratic function
b. Difference polynomial
c. Remez algorithm
d. Factor Theorem

11. In algebra, a _____ of an element in a quadratic extension field of a field K is its image under the unique non-identity automorphism of the extended field that fixes K. If the extension is generated by a square root of an element r of K, then the _____ of $a + b\sqrt{r}$ is $a - b\sqrt{r}$ for $a, b \in K$, and in particular in the case of the field C of complex numbers as an extension of the field R of real numbers (where r = − 1), the complex _____ of a + bi is a − bi.

Forming the sum or product of any element of the extension field with its _____ always gives an element of K. This can be used to rewrite a quotient of numbers in the extended field so that the denominator lies in K, by multiplying numerator and denominator by the _____ of the denominator. This process is called rationalization of the denominator, in particular if K is the field Q of rational numbers.

a. Field arithmetic
b. Digital root
c. K-theory
d. Conjugate

12. In mathematics, _____ or factoring is the decomposition of an object ' href='/wiki/Matrix_(mathematics)'>matrix) into a product of other objects, or factors, which when multiplied together give the original. For example, the number 15 factors into primes as 3 × 5, and the polynomial $x^2 - 4$ factors as (x − 2)(x + 2.) In all cases, a product of simpler objects is obtained.
a. -equivalence
b. 2-bridge knot
c. Factorization
d. -module

13. In mathematics, the word _____ is a term for any well-formed combination of mathematical symbols. For example,

$x^2 + 3x - 4$

is an _____, while

)x) / 0

is not, because the parentheses are not balanced and division by zero is undefined.

Being an _____ is a syntactic concept - the meaning of the variables is irrelevant, but different fields have different notions of validity.â€¢See formal language for how expressions are constructed, and formal semantics for meaning.

a. Expression
b. Arity
c. Unit ring
d. Orthogonal

14. In mathematics, especially in the area of abstract algebra known as ring theory, a _____ is a ring with $0 \neq 1$ such that $ab = 0$ implies that either $a = 0$ or $b = 0$ (the zero-product property.) That is, it is a nontrivial ring without left or right zero divisors. A commutative _____ is called an integral _____.

a. Subring
b. Partially-ordered ring
c. Domain
d. Coherent ring

15. In mathematics, a _____ is any function which can be written as the ratio of two polynomial functions. _____ of degree 2 : $y = \dfrac{x^2 - 3x - 2}{x^2 - 4}$

In the case of one variable, x, a _____ is a function of the form

$$f(x) = \dfrac{P(x)}{Q(x)}$$

where P and Q are polynomial function in x and Q is not the zero polynomial. The domain of f is the set of all points x for which the denominator Q(x) is not zero.

Chapter 4. Polynomial and Rational Functions 45

a. Legendre rational functions
b. -module
c. -equivalence
d. Rational function

16. An _____ is a pointed projectile that is shot with a bow. It predates recorded history and is common to most cultures. Schematic of an _____ with many parts.

A normal _____ consists of a shaft with an arrowhead attached to the front end, with fletchings and a nock at the other.

a. Abelian P-root group
b. Arrow
c. ADE classification
d. AKS primality test

17. In mathematics, the _____ of a real number is its numerical value without regard to its sign. So, for example, 3 is the _____ of both 3 and −3.

The _____ of a number a is denoted by $|a|$.

a. ADE classification
b. Abelian P-root group
c. AKS primality test
d. Absolute value

18. In mathematics, the (formal) _____ of a complex vector space V is the complex vector space $\overline{V}$ consisting of all formal complex conjugates of elements of V. That is, $\overline{V}$ is a vector space whose elements are in one-to-one correspondence with the elements of V:

$$\overline{V} = \{\overline{v} \mid v \in V\},$$

with the following rules for addition and scalar multiplication:

$$\overline{v} + \overline{w} = \overline{v + w} \quad \text{and} \quad \alpha \overline{v} = \overline{\overline{\alpha} v}.$$

Here v and w are vectors in V, α is a complex number, and $\overline{\alpha}$ denotes the _____ of α.

In the case where V is a linear subspace of $\mathbb{C}^n$, the formal _____ $\overline{V}$ is naturally isomorphic to the actual _____ subspace of V in $\mathbb{C}^n$.

a. Binomial inverse theorem
b. Polynomial basis
c. Conjugate transpose
d. Complex conjugate

19. In elementary algebra, a _____ is a polynomial with two terms--the sum of two monomials--often bound by parenthesis or brackets when operated upon. It is the simplest kind of polynomial other than monomials.

- The _____ $a^2 - b^2$ can be factored as the product of two other binomials:

    $a^2 - b^2 = (a + b)(a - b.)$

    This is a special case of the more general formula:
    $$a^{n+1} - b^{n+1} = (a-b)\sum_{k=0}^{n} a^k b^{n-k}$$

- The product of a pair of linear binomials (ax + b) and (cx + d) is:

    $(ax + b)(cx + d) = acx^2 + axd + bcx + bd.$

- A _____ raised to the nth power, represented as

    $(a + b)^n$
    can be expanded by means of the _____ theorem or, equivalently, using Pascal's triangle. Taking a simple example, the perfect square _____ $(p + q)^2$ can be found by squaring the :first digit, adding twice the product of the first and second digit and finally adding the square of the second digit, to give $p^2 + 2pq + q^2$.

a. Content
b. Theory of equations
c. Generalized arithmetic progression
d. Binomial

20. In mathematics, the _____ is an important formula giving the expansion of powers of sums. Its simplest version states that

$$(x+y)^n = \sum_{k=0}^{n} \binom{n}{k} x^{n-k} y^k \qquad (1)$$

for any real or complex numbers x and y, and any non-negative integer n. The binomial coefficient appearing in (1) may be defined in terms of the factorial function n!:

$$\binom{n}{k} = \frac{n!}{k!\,(n-k)!}.$$

For example, here are the cases where 2 ≤ n ≤ 5:

$$(x+y)^2 = x^2 + 2xy + y^2$$
$$(x+y)^3 = x^3 + 3x^2y + 3xy^2 + y^3$$
$$(x+y)^4 = x^4 + 4x^3y + 6x^2y^2 + 4xy^3 + y^4$$
$$(x+y)^5 = x^5 + 5x^4y + 10x^3y^2 + 10x^2y^3 + 5xy^4 + y^5.$$

Formula (1) is valid more generally for any elements x and y of a semiring as long as xy = yx.

a. -equivalence
b. Binomial Theorem
c. -module
d. 2-bridge knot

21. In mathematics, a _____ is a polynomial equation of the second degree. The general form is

$$ax^2 + bx + c = 0$$

The quadratic coefficient a is the coefficient of x^2, the linear coefficient b is the coefficient of x, and c is the constant coefficient, also called the free term or constant term.

Quadratic equations are called quadratic because the variable in the leading term is squared.

a. Quadratic equation
b. Difference of two squares
c. Rationalisation
d. Cubic function

Chapter 5. Exponential and Logarithmic Functions

1. In linear algebra, a _____ is a linear transformation that squares to the identity ($R^2 = I$, where R is in K dimensional space), also known as an involution in the general linear group. In addition to reflections across hyperplanes, the class of general reflections includes point reflections, reflections across subspaces of intermediate dimension, and non-orthogonal reflections.

A _____ over a hyperplane in an inner product space is necessarily symmetric, but a general _____ need not be as the example $\begin{bmatrix} 1 & 0 \\ 1 & -1 \end{bmatrix}$ shows.

   a. Morphism
   b. Reflection
   c. Homomorphic secret sharing
   d. Shear mappings

2. In mathematics, an _____ is the finite or bounded case of a conic section, the geometric shape that results from cutting a circular conical or cylindrical surface with an oblique plane. It is also the locus of all points of the plane whose distances to two fixed points add to the same constant.

Ellipses also arise as images of a circle or a sphere under parallel projection, and some cases of perspective projection.

   a. ADE classification
   b. Ellipse
   c. Abelian P-root group
   d. AKS primality test

Chapter 5. Exponential and Logarithmic Functions

3. In elementary algebra, a _____ is a polynomial with two terms--the sum of two monomials--often bound by parenthesis or brackets when operated upon. It is the simplest kind of polynomial other than monomials.

- The _____ a² - b² can be factored as the product of two other binomials:

    a² - b² = (a + b)(a - b.)

    This is a special case of the more general formula:
    $$a^{n+1} - b^{n+1} = (a-b)\sum_{k=0}^{n} a^k b^{n-k}$$

- The product of a pair of linear binomials (ax + b) and (cx + d) is:

    (ax + b)(cx + d) = acx² + axd + bcx + bd.

- A _____ raised to the nth power, represented as

    (a + b)^n

    can be expanded by means of the _____ theorem or, equivalently, using Pascal's triangle. Taking a simple example, the perfect square _____ (p + q)² can be found by squaring the :first digit, adding twice the product of the first and second digit and finally adding the square of the second digit, to give p² + 2pq + q².

a. Theory of equations
b. Binomial
c. Generalized arithmetic progression
d. Content

4. In mathematics, the _____ is an important formula giving the expansion of powers of sums. Its simplest version states that

$$(x+y)^n = \sum_{k=0}^{n} \binom{n}{k} x^{n-k} y^k \qquad (1)$$

for any real or complex numbers x and y, and any non-negative integer n. The binomial coefficient appearing in (1) may be defined in terms of the factorial function n!:

$$\binom{n}{k} = \frac{n!}{k!\,(n-k)!}.$$

For example, here are the cases where 2 ≤ n ≤ 5:

$$(x+y)^2 = x^2 + 2xy + y^2$$
$$(x+y)^3 = x^3 + 3x^2y + 3xy^2 + y^3$$
$$(x+y)^4 = x^4 + 4x^3y + 6x^2y^2 + 4xy^3 + y^4$$
$$(x+y)^5 = x^5 + 5x^4y + 10x^3y^2 + 10x^2y^3 + 5xy^4 + y^5.$$

Formula (1) is valid more generally for any elements x and y of a semiring as long as xy = yx.

a. -equivalence
b. 2-bridge knot
c. -module
d. Binomial Theorem

5. In mathematics, a _____ is a number that can be expressed as an integral of an algebraic function over an algebraic domain. The concept has been promoted by Maxim Kontsevich and Don Zagier.

In elementary mathematics each group of three digits in a number is called a _____

a. 2-bridge knot
b. -equivalence
c. Period
d. -module

6. Any formula written in terms of logarithms may be said to be in _____.

In contexts including complex manifolds and algebraic geometry, a logarithmic differential form is a 1-form that, locally at least, can be written

$$\frac{df}{f}$$

for some meromorphic function (resp. rational function) f.

a. Bispectrum
b. Meromorphic function
c. Hankel contour
d. Logarithmic form

7. In mathematics, especially in the area of abstract algebra known as ring theory, a _____ is a ring with 0 ≠ 1 such that ab = 0 implies that either a = 0 or b = 0 (the zero-product property.) That is, it is a nontrivial ring without left or right zero divisors. A commutative _____ is called an integral _____.
   a. Subring
   b. Partially-ordered ring
   c. Domain
   d. Coherent ring

8. In mathematics, the word _____ is a term for any well-formed combination of mathematical symbols. For example,

   $x^2 + 3x - 4$

is an _____, while

)x) / 0

is not, because the parentheses are not balanced and division by zero is undefined.

Being an _____ is a syntactic concept - the meaning of the variables is irrelevant, but different fields have different notions of validity.â€¢See formal language for how expressions are constructed, and formal semantics for meaning.

   a. Arity
   b. Unit ring
   c. Orthogonal
   d. Expression

9. In group theory, the _____ of a group with respect to a symmetric generating set describes the size of balls in the group. Every element in the group can be written as a product of generators, and the _____ counts the number of elements that can be written as a product of length n.

Suppose G is a finitely generated group; and T is a finite symmetric set of generators (symmetric means that if $x \in T$ then $x^{-1} \in T$.)

a. Z-group
b. Free-by-cyclic
c. Tits alternative
d. Growth rate

10. In a totally ordered set all elements are mutually comparable, so such a set can have at most one minimal element and at most one maximal element. Then, due to mutual comparability, the minimal element will also be the least element and the maximal element will also be the greatest element. Thus in a totally ordered set we can simply use the terms _____ and maximum.

a. Minimum
b. 2-bridge knot
c. -equivalence
d. -module

11. In mathematics, a _____ is a constant multiplicative factor of a certain object. For example, in the expression $9x^2$, the _____ of x^2 is 9.

The object can be such things as a variable, a vector, a function, etc.

a. Vandermonde polynomial
b. Coefficient
c. Constant term
d. Tschirnhaus transformation

Chapter 6. Systems of Equations and Inequalities

1. In mathematics, a _____ is a collection of linear equations involving the same set of variables. For example,

$$3x + 2y - z = 1$$
$$2x - 2y + 4z = -2$$
$$-x + \tfrac{1}{2}y - z = 0$$

is a system of three equations in the three variables x, y, z. A solution to a linear system is an assignment of numbers to the variables such that all the equations are simultaneously satisfied.

   a. Simultaneous equations
   b. -equivalence
   c. -module
   d. System of linear equations

2. In mathematics, a (B, N) _____ is a structure on groups of Lie type that allows one to give uniform proofs of many results, instead of giving a large number of case-by-case proofs. Roughly speaking, it shows that all such groups are similar to the general linear group over a field. They were invented by the mathematician Jacques Tits, and are also sometimes known as Tits systems.
   a. Pair
   b. Group representations
   c. Group action
   d. Rank of a group

3. In linear algebra, _____ is an efficient algorithm for solving systems of linear equations, finding the rank of a matrix, and calculating the inverse of an invertible square matrix. _____ is named after German mathematician and scientist Carl Friedrich Gauss.

Elementary row operations are used to reduce a matrix to row echelon form.

   a. -equivalence
   b. 2-bridge knot
   c. -module
   d. Gaussian elimination

4. A _____ is a symbol that stands for a value that may vary; the term usually occurs in opposition to constant, which is a symbol for a non-varying value, i.e. completely fixed or fixed in the context of use. The concepts of constants and variables are fundamental to all modern mathematics, science, engineering, and computer programming.

Chapter 6. Systems of Equations and Inequalities

Much of the basic theory for which we use variables today, such as school geometry and algebra, was developed thousands of years ago, but the use of symbolic formulae and variables is only several hundreds of years old.

a. Variable
b. -module
c. -equivalence
d. 2-bridge knot

5. _____ is the mathematical process of putting things together. The plus sign '+' means that numbers are added together. For example, in the picture on the right, there are 3 + 2 apples--meaning three apples and two other apples--which is the same as five apples, since 3 + 2 = 5.

a. Abelian P-root group
b. AKS primality test
c. ADE classification
d. Addition

6. In mathematics, and more specifically set theory, the _____ is the unique set having no (zero) members. Some axiomatic set theories assure that the _____ exists by including an axiom of _____; in other theories, its existence can be deduced. Many possible properties of sets are trivially true for the _____.

a. Empty set
b. Abelian P-root group
c. ADE classification
d. AKS primality test

7. In mathematics, the _____ of a real number is its numerical value without regard to its sign. So, for example, 3 is the _____ of both 3 and −3.

The _____ of a number a is denoted by $|a|$.

a. ADE classification
b. AKS primality test
c. Abelian P-root group
d. Absolute value

8. A _____, in mathematics, is a polynomial function of the form f(x) = ax² + bx + c = 0, where $a \neq 0$. The graph of a _____ is a parabola whose major axis is parallel to the y-axis.

The expression ax² + bx + c in the definition of a _____ is a polynomial of degree 2 or second order, or a 2nd degree polynomial, because the highest exponent of x is 2.

   a. Factor theorem
   b. Quadratic function
   c. Dickson polynomials
   d. Vandermonde polynomial

9. In mathematics, a _____ is any function which can be written as the ratio of two polynomial functions. _____ of degree 2 : $y = \dfrac{x^2 - 3x - 2}{x^2 - 4}$

In the case of one variable, x, a _____ is a function of the form

$$f(x) = \frac{P(x)}{Q(x)}$$

where P and Q are polynomial function in x and Q is not the zero polynomial. The domain of f is the set of all points x for which the denominator Q(x) is not zero.

   a. -equivalence
   b. -module
   c. Legendre rational functions
   d. Rational function

10. In mathematics, an _____ is the finite or bounded case of a conic section, the geometric shape that results from cutting a circular conical or cylindrical surface with an oblique plane . It is also the locus of all points of the plane whose distances to two fixed points add to the same constant.

Ellipses also arise as images of a circle or a sphere under parallel projection, and some cases of perspective projection.

   a. ADE classification
   b. AKS primality test
   c. Abelian P-root group
   d. Ellipse

Chapter 6. Systems of Equations and Inequalities

11. In mathematics, a _____ is a bijection between skew diagrams satisfying certain properties, introduced by Zelevinsky (1981) in a generalization of the Robinson-Schensted correspondence and the Littlewood-Richardson rule.
    a. -equivalence
    b. Picture
    c. -module
    d. Macdonald polynomials

12. In mathematics, a _____ or reciprocal for a number x, denoted by $\frac{1}{x}$ or x^{-1}, is a number which when multiplied by x yields the multiplicative identity, 1. The _____ of x is also called the reciprocal of x. The _____ of a fraction a/b is b/a.
    a. -equivalence
    b. Multiplicative inverse
    c. 2-bridge knot
    d. -module

13. In mathematics, the word _____ is a term for any well-formed combination of mathematical symbols. For example,

    $x^2 + 3x - 4$

is an _____, while

)x) / 0

is not, because the parentheses are not balanced and division by zero is undefined.

Being an _____ is a syntactic concept - the meaning of the variables is irrelevant, but different fields have different notions of validity.â€¢See formal language for how expressions are constructed, and formal semantics for meaning.

   a. Unit ring
   b. Orthogonal
   c. Expression
   d. Arity

Chapter 6. Systems of Equations and Inequalities

14. In mathematics, an _____ is a statement about the relative size or order of two objects, or about whether they are the same or not

    - The notation a < b means that a is less than b.
    - The notation a > b means that a is greater than b.
    - The notation a ≠ b means that a is not equal to b, but does not say that one is bigger than the other or even that they can be compared in size.

In all these cases, a is not equal to b, hence, '_____'.

These relations are known as strict _____

    - The notation a ≤ b means that a is less than or equal to b (or, equivalently, not greater than b);
    - The notation a ≥ b means that a is greater than or equal to b (or, equivalently, not smaller than b);

An additional use of the notation is to show that one quantity is much greater than another, normally by several orders of magnitude.

    - The notation a ≪ b means that a is much less than b.
    - The notation a ≫ b means that a is much greater than b.

If the sense of the _____ is the same for all values of the variables for which its members are defined, then the _____ is called an 'absolute' or 'unconditional' _____. If the sense of an _____ holds only for certain values of the variables involved, but is reversed or destroyed for other values of the variables, it is called a conditional _____.

One can apply the same algebraic operations to inequalities as one would apply for solving equalities. For example, to find x for the _____ 10x > 20 one would divide 20 by 10 to obtain x > 2.

   a. Abelian P-root group
   b. ADE classification
   c. Inequality
   d. AKS primality test

15. If the space is two-dimensional, then a half-space is called a _____ A half-space in a one-dimensional space is called a ray.

A half-space may be specified by a linear inequality, derived from the linear equation that specifies the defining hyperplane.

a. Half-plane
b. -module
c. 2-bridge knot
d. -equivalence

16. In mathematics, _____ is a technique for optimization of a linear objective function, subject to linear equality and linear inequality constraints. Informally, _____ determines the way to achieve the best outcome (such as maximum profit or lowest cost) in a given mathematical model and given some list of requirements represented as linear equations.

More formally, given a polytope (for example, a polygon or a polyhedron), and a real-valued affine function

$$f(x_1, x_2, \ldots, x_n) = c_1 x_1 + c_2 x_2 + \cdots + c_n x_n + d$$

defined on this polytope, a _____ method will find a point in the polytope where this function has the smallest (or largest) value.

a. 2-bridge knot
b. -module
c. -equivalence
d. Linear programming

17. In set theory, the term _____ refers to a set operation used in the convergence of set elements to form a resultant set containing the elements of both sets. As a simple example, a _____ of two disjoint sets, which do not have elements in common results in a set containing all elements from both sets. A Venn diagram representing the _____ of sets A and B. If one circle represents A, and the other B, then the red area represents the _____ of A and B. The area where the circles join, also shown in red, is the intersection of the two sets.

If we define two sets which contain unique elements; those of A not occurring in B and vice versa, then the _____ of these sets results in a set which contains all elements of A and B. In terms of notation, we could define this set operation as the following:

A = {1,2,3,4}
B = {5,6,7,8}
$$A \cup B = \{1, 2, 3, 4, 5, 6, 7, 8\}$$

Other more complex operations can be done including the _____, if the set is for example defined by a property rather than a finite or assumed infinite enumeration of elements.

a. ADE classification
b. AKS primality test
c. Abelian P-root group
d. Union

18. In mathematics, a _____ is a rectangular array of numbers. This way, matrices can record data that depend on multiple parameters. In particular they are used to keep track of the coefficients of multiple linear equations. Matrices are closely connected to linear transformations, which are higher-dimensional analogs of linear functions, i.e., functions of the form f(x) = c Â· x, where c is a constant. This map corresponds to a _____ with one row and column, with entry c. In addition to a number of elementary, entrywise operations such as _____ addition a key notion is _____ multiplication, which displays a number of features not encountered in numbers; for example, products of matrices depend on the order of the factors, unlike products of real numbers, say, where c Â· d = d Â· c for any two numbers c and d.
   a. Heap
   b. Polynomial expression
   c. Commutativity
   d. Matrix

Chapter 7. Matrices and Determinants

1. In linear algebra, the _____ of a matrix is obtained by changing a matrix in some way.

Given the matrices A and B, where:

$$A = \begin{bmatrix} 1 & 3 & 2 \\ 2 & 0 & 1 \\ 5 & 2 & 2 \end{bmatrix}, \quad B = \begin{bmatrix} 4 \\ 3 \\ 1 \end{bmatrix}$$

Then, the _____ is written as:

$$(A|B) = \begin{bmatrix} 1 & 3 & 2 & 4 \\ 2 & 0 & 1 & 3 \\ 5 & 2 & 2 & 1 \end{bmatrix}$$

This is useful when solving systems of linear equations or the _____ may also be used to find the inverse of a matrix by combining it with the identity matrix.

Let C be a square 2×2 matrix where $$C = \begin{bmatrix} 1 & 3 \\ -5 & 0 \end{bmatrix}$$

To find the inverse of C we create (C|I) where I is the 2×2 identity matrix.

a. Euclidean distance matrix
b. Augmented matrix
c. Unistochastic matrix
d. Unitary matrix

2. In linear algebra, _____ is an efficient algorithm for solving systems of linear equations, finding the rank of a matrix, and calculating the inverse of an invertible square matrix. _____ is named after German mathematician and scientist Carl Friedrich Gauss.

Elementary row operations are used to reduce a matrix to row echelon form.

a. -module
b. 2-bridge knot
c. -equivalence
d. Gaussian elimination

3. In mathematics, a _____ is a collection of linear equations involving the same set of variables. For example,

Chapter 7. Matrices and Determinants 61

$$3x + 2y - z = 1$$
$$2x - 2y + 4z = -2$$
$$-x + \tfrac{1}{2}y - z = 0$$

is a system of three equations in the three variables x, y, z. A solution to a linear system is an assignment of numbers to the variables such that all the equations are simultaneously satisfied.

a. -equivalence
b. Simultaneous equations
c. -module
d. System of linear equations

4. In mathematics, a _____ is a rectangular array of numbers. This way, matrices can record data that depend on multiple parameters. In particular they are used to keep track of the coefficients of multiple linear equations. Matrices are closely connected to linear transformations, which are higher-dimensional analogs of linear functions, i.e., functions of the form f(x) = c · x, where c is a constant. This map corresponds to a _____ with one row and column, with entry c. In addition to a number of elementary, entrywise operations such as _____ addition a key notion is _____ multiplication, which displays a number of features not encountered in numbers; for example, products of matrices depend on the order of the factors, unlike products of real numbers, say, where c · d = d · c for any two numbers c and d.
   a. Matrix
   b. Heap
   c. Commutativity
   d. Polynomial expression

5. In its simplest meaning in mathematics and logic, an _____ is an action or procedure which produces a new value from one or more input values. There are two common types of operations: unary and binary. Unary operations involve only one value, such as negation and trigonometric functions.
   a. ADE classification
   b. AKS primality test
   c. Abelian P-root group
   d. Operation

6. A _____ is a symbol that stands for a value that may vary; the term usually occurs in opposition to constant, which is a symbol for a non-varying value, i.e. completely fixed or fixed in the context of use. The concepts of constants and variables are fundamental to all modern mathematics, science, engineering, and computer programming.

Much of the basic theory for which we use variables today, such as school geometry and algebra, was developed thousands of years ago, but the use of symbolic formulae and variables is only several hundreds of years old.

a. -module
b. -equivalence
c. 2-bridge knot
d. Variable

7. In group theory, a branch of mathematics, the term _____ is used in two closely related senses:

- the _____ of a group is its cardinality, i.e. the number of its elements;
- the _____, sometimes period, of an element a of a group is the smallest positive integer m such that a^m = e (where e denotes the identity element of the group, and a^m denotes the product of m copies of a.) If no such m exists, we say that a has infinite _____. All elements of finite groups have finite _____.

We denote the _____ of a group G by ord(G) or $|G|$ and the _____ of an element a by ord(a) or $|a|$.

Example. The symmetric group S_3 has the following multiplication table.

This group has six elements, so ord(S_3) = 6.

a. Artin group
b. Index calculus algorithm
c. Outer automorphism group
d. Order

8. _____ is the mathematical process of putting things together. The plus sign '+' means that numbers are added together. For example, in the picture on the right, there are 3 + 2 apples--meaning three apples and two other apples--which is the same as five apples, since 3 + 2 = 5.

a. Addition
b. Abelian P-root group
c. AKS primality test
d. ADE classification

9. _____ is one of the four basic arithmetic operations; it is the inverse of addition, meaning that if we start with any number and add any number and then subtract the same number we added, we return to the number we started with. _____ is denoted by a minus sign in infix notation.

Chapter 7. Matrices and Determinants 63

The traditional names for the parts of the formula

    c − b = a

are minuend (c) − subtrahend (b) = difference (a.)

a. -module
b. -equivalence
c. 2-bridge knot
d. Subtraction

10. In mathematics the _____ of a set which is equipped with the operation of addition is an element which, when added to any element x in the set, yields x. One of the most familiar additive identities is the number 0 from elementary mathematics, but additive identities occur in other mathematical structures where addition is defined, such as in groups and rings.

- The _____ familiar from elementary mathematics is zero, denoted 0. For example,

    5 + 0 = 5 = 0 + 5.

- In the natural numbers N and all of its supersets (the integers Z, the rational numbers Q, the real numbers R, or the complex numbers C), the _____ is 0. Thus for any one of these numbers n,

    n + 0 = n = 0 + n.

Let N be a set which is closed under the operation of addition, denoted +. An _____ for N is any element e such that for any element n in N,

    e + n = n = n + e.

a. Universal algebra
b. Identity element
c. External
d. Additive identity

11. In algebra, a commutative ring R is said to be _____ if any of the following equivalent conditions holds:

1. The localization $R_\mathfrak{m}$ of R at $\mathfrak{m}$ is a valuation ring for every maximal ideal $\mathfrak{m}$ of R.
2. For all ideals $\mathfrak{a}$, $\mathfrak{b}$, and $\mathfrak{c}$,

$$a \cap (b+c) = (a \cap b) + (a \cap c)$$

- For all ideals a, b, and c,

$$a + (b \cap c) = (a+b) \cap (a+c)$$

An _____ domain is called a Prüfer domain.

a. Inverse eigenvalues theorem
b. Ordered vector space
c. Exchange matrix
d. Arithmetical

12. In mathematics, _____ is the operation of adding two matrices by adding the corresponding entries together. However, there is another operation which could also be considered as a kind of addition for matrices.

The usual _____ is defined for two matrices of the same dimensions.

a. Nonlinear eigenproblem
b. Projection-valued measure
c. Matrix addition
d. Cofactor

13. In mathematics, the _____ of a number n is the number that, when added to n, yields zero. The _____ of F is denoted −F.

For example, the _____ of 7 is −7, because 7 + (−7) = 0, and the _____ of −0.3 is 0.3, because −0.3 + 0.3 = 0.

a. Artinian ideal
b. Isomorphism class
c. Interior algebra
d. Additive inverse

14. The real component of a quaternion is also called its _____ part.

Chapter 7. Matrices and Determinants

The term is also sometimes used informally to mean a vector, matrix, tensor, or other usually 'compound' value that is actually reduced to a single component. Thus, for example, the product of a 1×n matrix and an n×1 matrix, which is formally a 1×1 matrix, is often said to be a _____.

   a. Scalar
   b. Self-adjoint
   c. Tensor product
   d. Distributivity

15. In mathematics, _____ is one of the basic operations defining a vector space in linear algebra Note that _____ is different from scalar product which is an inner product between two vectors.

More specifically, if K is a field and V is a vector space over K, then _____ is a function from K × V to V. The result of applying this function to c in K and v in V is denoted cv.

   a. Scalar multiplication
   b. Symplectic vector space
   c. K-frame
   d. Matrix pencil

16. In mathematics, a _____ is a polynomial equation of the second degree. The general form is

$$ax^2 + bx + c = 0$$

The quadratic coefficient a is the coefficient of x^2, the linear coefficient b is the coefficient of x, and c is the constant coefficient, also called the free term or constant term.

Quadratic equations are called quadratic because the variable in the leading term is squared.

   a. Rationalisation
   b. Quadratic equation
   c. Cubic function
   d. Difference of two squares

17. In mathematics, the _____ is a matrix function on square matrices analogous to the ordinary exponential function. Abstractly, the _____ gives the connection between a matrix Lie algebra and the corresponding Lie group.

Let X be an n×n real or complex matrix.

a. -module
b. 2-bridge knot
c. Matrix Exponential
d. -equivalence

18. _____ is the subject area of mathematics that studies algebraic structures, such as groups, rings, fields, modules, vector spaces, and algebras. The phrase _____ was coined at the turn of the 20th century to distinguish this area from what was normally referred to as algebra, the study of the rules for manipulating formulas and algebraic expressions involving unknowns and real or complex numbers, often now called elementary algebra. The distinction is rarely made in more recent writings.
   a. Fibonacci
   b. Blue sky catastrophe
   c. Inverse function
   d. Abstract algebra

19. In mathematics, an _____ is the finite or bounded case of a conic section, the geometric shape that results from cutting a circular conical or cylindrical surface with an oblique plane . It is also the locus of all points of the plane whose distances to two fixed points add to the same constant.

Ellipses also arise as images of a circle or a sphere under parallel projection, and some cases of perspective projection.

   a. Abelian P-root group
   b. ADE classification
   c. Ellipse
   d. AKS primality test

20. In linear algebra, the _____ or unit matrix of size n is the n-by-n square matrix with ones on the main diagonal and zeros elsewhere. It is denoted by I_n, or simply by I if the size is immaterial or can be trivially determined by the context. (In some fields, such as quantum mechanics, the _____ is denoted by a boldface one, 1; otherwise it is identical to I.)
   a. Orthogonal
   b. Associativity
   c. Artinian ideal
   d. Identity matrix

21. In mathematics, a _____ or reciprocal for a number x, denoted by $1/x$ or x^{-1}, is a number which when multiplied by x yields the multiplicative identity, 1. The _____ of x is also called the reciprocal of x. The _____ of a fraction a/b is b/a.

a. -equivalence
b. Multiplicative inverse
c. 2-bridge knot
d. -module

22. Let S be a set with a binary operation * . If e is an identity element of (S, *) and a * b = e, then a is called a _____ of b and b is called a right inverse of a. If an element x is both a _____ and a right inverse of y, then x is called a two-sided inverse, or simply an inverse, of y.
   a. -module
   b. 2-bridge knot
   c. -equivalence
   d. Left inverse

23. If $A_1, A_2, ..., A_n$ are _____ square matrices over a field, then

$$(A_1 A_2 \cdots A_n)^{-1} = A_n^{-1} A_{n-1}^{-1} \cdots A_1^{-1}.$$

It becomes evident why this is the case if one attempts to find an inverse for the product of the A_is from first principles, that is, that we wish to determine B such that

$$(A_1 A_2 \cdots A_n) B = I$$

where B is the inverse matrix of the product. To remove A_1 from the product, we can then write

$$A_1^{-1} (A_1 A_2 \cdots A_n) B = A_1^{-1} I$$

which would reduce the equation to

$$(A_2 A_3 \cdots A_n) B = A_1^{-1} I.$$

Likewise, then, from

$$A_2^{-1} (A_2 A_3 \cdots A_n) B = A_2^{-1} A_1^{-1} I$$

which simplifies to

$$(A_3 A_4 \cdots A_n) B = A_2^{-1} A_1^{-1} I.$$

If one repeat the process up to A_n, the equation becomes

$$B = A_n^{-1}A_{n-1}^{-1} \cdots A_2^{-1}A_1^{-1}I$$

$$B = A_n^{-1}A_{n-1}^{-1} \cdots A_2^{-1}A_1^{-1}$$

but B is the inverse matrix, i.e. $B = (A_1 A_2 \cdots A_n)^{-1}$ so the property is established.

Over the field of real numbers, the set of singular n-by-n matrices, considered as a subset of $R^{n \times n}$, is a null set, i.e., has Lebesgue measure zero.

a. -module
b. -equivalence
c. 2-bridge knot
d. Nonsingular

24. Matrix inversion is the process of finding the matrix B that satisfies the prior equation for a given _____ A.
a. Overdetermined
b. Orientation
c. Invertible matrix
d. Independent equation

25. In mathematics, a _____ is a constant multiplicative factor of a certain object. For example, in the expression $9x^2$, the _____ of x^2 is 9.

The object can be such things as a variable, a vector, a function, etc.

a. Tschirnhaus transformation
b. Vandermonde polynomial
c. Coefficient
d. Constant term

26. In linear algebra, the _____ refers to a matrix consisting of the coefficients of the variables in a set of linear equations.

Chapter 7. Matrices and Determinants

In general, a system with m linear equations and n unknowns can be written as

$$a_{11}x_1 + a_{12}x_2 + ... + a_{1n}x_n = b_1$$
$$a_{21}x_1 + a_{22}x_2 + ... + a_{2n}x_n = b_2$$
$$\vdots$$
$$a_{m1}x_1 + a_{m2}x_2 + ... + a_{mn}x_n = b_m$$

where $x_1, x_2, ..., x_n$ are the unknowns and the numbers $a_{11}, a_{12}, ..., a_{mn}$ are the coefficients of the system. The _____ is the mxn matrix with the coefficient a_{ij} as the (i,j)-th entry:

$$\begin{bmatrix} a_{11} & a_{12} & \cdots & a_{1n} \\ a_{21} & a_{22} & \cdots & a_{2n} \\ \vdots & \vdots & \ddots & \vdots \\ a_{m1} & a_{m2} & \cdots & a_{mn} \end{bmatrix}$$

a. Centrosymmetric matrix
b. Segre classification
c. Linear inequality
d. Coefficient matrix

27. In algebra, a _____ is a function depending on n that associates a scalar, det(A), to an n×n square matrix A. The fundamental geometric meaning of a _____ is a scale factor for measure when A is regarded as a linear transformation. Determinants are important both in calculus, where they enter the substitution rule for several variables, and in multilinear algebra.

For a fixed nonnegative integer n, there is a unique _____ function for the n×n matrices over any commutative ring R. In particular, this function exists when R is the field of real or complex numbers.

a. Determinant
b. Leibniz formula
c. Functional determinant
d. Pfaffian

28. In mathematics, an _____ of a product of sums expresses it as a sum of products by using the fact that multiplication distributes over addition. Expansions of polynomials are obtained by multiplying together their factors, which results in a sum of terms with variables raised to different degrees.

Chapter 7. Matrices and Determinants

To multiply two factors, each term of the first factor must be multiplied by each term of the other factor.

a. Analytic subgroup
b. Ordered vector space
c. Equipotential surfaces
d. Expansion

29. In linear algebra, a _____ of a matrix A is the determinant of some smaller square matrix, cut down from A by removing one or more of its rows or columns. Minors obtained by removing just one row and one column from square matrices (first minors) are required for calculating matrix cofactors, which in turn are useful for computing both the determinant and inverse of square matrices.

a. Minor
b. Rng
c. Purification
d. Supergroup

30. In elementary algebra, a _____ is a polynomial with two terms--the sum of two monomials--often bound by parenthesis or brackets when operated upon. It is the simplest kind of polynomial other than monomials.

- The _____ $a^2 - b^2$ can be factored as the product of two other binomials:

    $a^2 - b^2 = (a + b)(a - b.)$

    $$a^{n+1} - b^{n+1} = (a - b) \sum_{k=0}^{n} a^k b^{n-k}$$

    This is a special case of the more general formula:

- The product of a pair of linear binomials (ax + b) and (cx + d) is:

    $(ax + b)(cx + d) = acx^2 + axd + bcx + bd.$

- A _____ raised to the nth power, represented as

    $(a + b)^n$

    can be expanded by means of the _____ theorem or, equivalently, using Pascal's triangle. Taking a simple example, the perfect square _____ $(p + q)^2$ can be found by squaring the :first digit, adding twice the product of the first and second digit and finally adding the square of the second digit, to give $p^2 + 2pq + q^2$.

Chapter 7. Matrices and Determinants

a. Content
b. Theory of equations
c. Generalized arithmetic progression
d. Binomial

31. In mathematics, the _____ is an important formula giving the expansion of powers of sums. Its simplest version states that

$$(x+y)^n = \sum_{k=0}^{n} \binom{n}{k} x^{n-k} y^k \qquad (1)$$

for any real or complex numbers x and y, and any non-negative integer n. The binomial coefficient appearing in (1) may be defined in terms of the factorial function n!:

$$\binom{n}{k} = \frac{n!}{k!(n-k)!}.$$

For example, here are the cases where $2 \leq n \leq 5$:

$$(x+y)^2 = x^2 + 2xy + y^2$$
$$(x+y)^3 = x^3 + 3x^2y + 3xy^2 + y^3$$
$$(x+y)^4 = x^4 + 4x^3y + 6x^2y^2 + 4xy^3 + y^4$$
$$(x+y)^5 = x^5 + 5x^4y + 10x^3y^2 + 10x^2y^3 + 5xy^4 + y^5.$$

Formula (1) is valid more generally for any elements x and y of a semiring as long as xy = yx.

a. -equivalence
b. -module
c. 2-bridge knot
d. Binomial Theorem

Chapter 8. Conic Sections and Analytic Geometry

1. In mathematics, a _____ is a curve obtained by intersecting a cone (more precisely, a circular conical surface) with a plane. A _____ is therefore a restriction of a quadric surface to the plane. The conic sections were named and studied as long ago as 200 BC, when Apollonius of Perga undertook a systematic study of their properties.

    a. Derivation of the cartesian form for an ellipse
    b. Conic section
    c. Matrix representation of conic sections
    d. Dandelin spheres

2. In the mathematical field of topology, a _____ of a fiber bundle, π: E → B, over a topological space, B, is a continuous map, s : B → E, such that π(s(x))=x for all x in B.

    A _____ is a certain generalization of the notion of the graph of a function. The graph of a function g : X → Y can be identified with a function taking its values in the Cartesian product E = X×Y of X and Y:

    $$s(x) = (x, g(x)) \in E, \quad s : X \to E.$$

    A _____ is an abstract characterization of what it means to be a graph.

    a. Section
    b. -equivalence
    c. -module
    d. Fiber bundle

3. In mathematics, an _____ is the finite or bounded case of a conic section, the geometric shape that results from cutting a circular conical or cylindrical surface with an oblique plane . It is also the locus of all points of the plane whose distances to two fixed points add to the same constant.

    Ellipses also arise as images of a circle or a sphere under parallel projection, and some cases of perspective projection.

    a. AKS primality test
    b. Abelian P-root group
    c. ADE classification
    d. Ellipse

4. In mathematics, the _____ is a conic section, the intersection of a right circular conical surface and a plane parallel to a generating straight line of that surface. Given a point (the focus) and a line (the directrix) that lie in a plane, the locus of points in that plane that are equidistant to them is a _____.

    A particular case arises when the plane is tangent to the conical surface of a circle.

a. -module
b. 2-bridge knot
c. -equivalence
d. Parabola

5. The term _____ or centre is used in various contexts in abstract algebra to denote the set of all those elements that commute with all other elements. More specifically:

- The _____ of a group G consists of all those elements x in G such that xg = gx for all g in G. This is a normal subgroup of G.
- The _____ of a ring R is the subset of R consisting of all those elements x of R such that xr = rx for all r in R. The _____ is a commutative subring of R, so R is an algebra over its _____.
- The _____ of an algebra A consists of all those elements x of A such that xa = ax for all a in A. See also: central simple algebra.
- The _____ of a Lie algebra L consists of all those elements x in L such that [x,a] = 0 for all a in L. This is an ideal of the Lie algebra L.
- The _____ of a monoidal category C consists of pairs (A,u) where A is an object of C, and $u : A \otimes - \to - \otimes A$ a natural isomorphism satisfying certain axioms.

a. Self-adjoint
b. Left alternative
c. Ring theory
d. Center

6. In geometry, the foci, pronounced , are a pair of special points used in describing conic sections. The four types of conic sections are the circle, parabola, ellipse, and hyperbola.

The _____ has two equivalent defining properties; and they always fall on the major axis of symmetry of the conic.

a. Conic section
b. Dandelin spheres
c. Focus
d. Derivation of the cartesian form for an ellipse

7. In linear algebra, a _____ of a matrix A is the determinant of some smaller square matrix, cut down from A by removing one or more of its rows or columns. Minors obtained by removing just one row and one column from square matrices (first minors) are required for calculating matrix cofactors, which in turn are useful for computing both the determinant and inverse of square matrices.

a. Purification
b. Rng
c. Minor
d. Supergroup

8. In elementary algebra, _____ is a technique for converting a quadratic polynomial of the form

$$ax^2 + bx + c$$

to the form

$$a(\cdots\cdots)^2 + \text{constant}.$$

The expression inside the parenthesis is of the form x − constant. Thus one converts $ax^2 + bx + c$ to

$$a(x - h)^2 + k$$

and one must find h and k.

_____ is used in

- solving quadratic equations,
- graphing quadratic functions,
- evaluating integrals in calculus,
- finding Laplace transforms.

In mathematics, _____ is considered a basic algebraic operation, and is often applied without remark in any computation involving quadratic polynomials.

There is a simple formula in elementary algebra for computing the square of a binomial:

$$(x + p)^2 = x^2 + 2px + p^2.$$

For example:

$$(x + 3)^2 = x^2 + 6x + 9 \qquad (p = 3)$$
$$(x - 5)^2 = x^2 - 10x + 25 \qquad (p = -5).$$

In any perfect square, the number p is always half the coefficient of x, and then the constant term is equal to p^2.

a. Reduct
b. Content
c. Nested radical
d. Completing the square

9. In linear algebra, a _____ is a linear transformation that squares to the identity ($R^2 = I$, where R is in K dimensional space), also known as an involution in the general linear group. In addition to reflections across hyperplanes, the class of general reflections includes point reflections, reflections across subspaces of intermediate dimension, and non-orthogonal reflections.

A _____ over a hyperplane in an inner product space is necessarily symmetric, but a general _____ need not be as the example $\begin{bmatrix} 1 & 0 \\ 1 & -1 \end{bmatrix}$ shows.

a. Reflection
b. Homomorphic secret sharing
c. Morphism
d. Shear mappings

10. In algebra, a _____ of an element in a quadratic extension field of a field K is its image under the unique non-identity automorphism of the extended field that fixes K. If the extension is generated by a square root of an element r of K, then the _____ of $a + b\sqrt{r}$ is $a - b\sqrt{r}$ for $a, b \in K$, and in particular in the case of the field C of complex numbers as an extension of the field R of real numbers (where r = − 1), the complex _____ of a + bi is a − bi.

Forming the sum or product of any element of the extension field with its _____ always gives an element of K. This can be used to rewrite a quotient of numbers in the extended field so that the denominator lies in K, by multiplying numerator and denominator by the _____ of the denominator. This process is called rationalization of the denominator, in particular if K is the field Q of rational numbers.

a. Conjugate
b. Digital root
c. K-theory
d. Field arithmetic

11. In linear algebra, a _____ is a set of vectors that, in a linear combination, can represent every vector in a given vector space or free module, and such that no element of the set can be represented as a linear combination of the others. In other words, a _____ is a linearly independent spanning set.

a. Basis
b. Chirality
c. Supergroup
d. Minor

12. In geometry, a _____ is a straight curve. When geometry is used to model the real world, lines are used to represent straight objects with negligible width and height. Lines are an idealisation of such objects and have no width or height at all and are usually considered to be infinitely long.

   a. -equivalence
   b. -module
   c. 2-bridge knot
   d. Line

13. In mathematics, a _____ in a topological space X is a continuous map f from the unit interval I = [0,1] to X

   $f : I \to X$.

The initial point of the _____ is f(0) and the terminal point is f(1.) One often speaks of a '_____ from x to y' where x and y are the initial and terminal points of the _____.

   a. Genus
   b. Suspension
   c. Path
   d. Simplicial complex

14. In topology, especially algebraic topology, the _____ CX of a topological space X is the quotient space:

$$CX = (X \times I)/(X \times \{0\})$$

of the product of X with the unit interval I = [0, 1]. Intuitively we make X into a cylinder and collapse one end of the cylinder to a point.

If X sits inside Euclidean space, the _____ on X is homeomorphic to the union of lines from X to another point.

a. Cone
b. Descent
c. Smash product
d. Genus

Chapter 9. Sequences, Induction, and Probability

1. In mathematics, especially in the area of abstract algebra known as ring theory, a _____ is a ring with 0 ≠ 1 such that ab = 0 implies that either a = 0 or b = 0 (the zero-product property.) That is, it is a nontrivial ring without left or right zero divisors. A commutative _____ is called an integral _____.
    a. Partially-ordered ring
    b. Coherent ring
    c. Subring
    d. Domain

2. In algebra, a commutative ring R is said to be _____ if any of the following equivalent conditions holds:

    1. The localization $R_\mathfrak{m}$ of R at $\mathfrak{m}$ is a valuation ring for every maximal ideal $\mathfrak{m}$ of R.
    2. For all ideals $\mathfrak{a}, \mathfrak{b},$ and $\mathfrak{c}$,

    $$\mathfrak{a} \cap (\mathfrak{b} + \mathfrak{c}) = (\mathfrak{a} \cap \mathfrak{b}) + (\mathfrak{a} \cap \mathfrak{c})$$

    - For all ideals $\mathfrak{a}, \mathfrak{b},$ and $\mathfrak{c}$,

    $$\mathfrak{a} + (\mathfrak{b} \cap \mathfrak{c}) = (\mathfrak{a} + \mathfrak{b}) \cap (\mathfrak{a} + \mathfrak{c})$$

    An _____ domain is called a Prüfer domain.

    a. Exchange matrix
    b. Inverse eigenvalues theorem
    c. Ordered vector space
    d. Arithmetical

3. In elementary algebra, a _____ is a polynomial with two terms--the sum of two monomials--often bound by parenthesis or brackets when operated upon. It is the simplest kind of polynomial other than monomials.

- The _____ $a^2 - b^2$ can be factored as the product of two other binomials:

    $a^2 - b^2 = (a + b)(a - b.)$

    This is a special case of the more general formula:

    $$a^{n+1} - b^{n+1} = (a - b) \sum_{k=0}^{n} a^k b^{n-k}$$

- The product of a pair of linear binomials (ax + b) and (cx + d) is:

    $(ax + b)(cx + d) = acx^2 + axd + bcx + bd.$

- A _____ raised to the nth power, represented as

    $(a + b)^n$

    can be expanded by means of the _____ theorem or, equivalently, using Pascal's triangle. Taking a simple example, the perfect square _____ $(p + q)^2$ can be found by squaring the :first digit, adding twice the product of the first and second digit and finally adding the square of the second digit, to give $p^2 + 2pq + q^2$.

a. Content
b. Generalized arithmetic progression
c. Theory of equations
d. Binomial

4. In mathematics, the _____ is an important formula giving the expansion of powers of sums. Its simplest version states that

$$(x + y)^n = \sum_{k=0}^{n} \binom{n}{k} x^{n-k} y^k \qquad (1)$$

for any real or complex numbers x and y, and any non-negative integer n. The binomial coefficient appearing in (1) may be defined in terms of the factorial function n!:

$$\binom{n}{k} = \frac{n!}{k!\,(n-k)!}.$$

For example, here are the cases where 2 ≤ n ≤ 5:

$$(x+y)^2 = x^2 + 2xy + y^2$$
$$(x+y)^3 = x^3 + 3x^2y + 3xy^2 + y^3$$
$$(x+y)^4 = x^4 + 4x^3y + 6x^2y^2 + 4xy^3 + y^4$$
$$(x+y)^5 = x^5 + 5x^4y + 10x^3y^2 + 10x^2y^3 + 5xy^4 + y^5.$$

Formula (1) is valid more generally for any elements x and y of a semiring as long as xy = yx.

- a. -equivalence
- b. -module
- c. 2-bridge knot
- d. Binomial Theorem

5. In mathematics, an _____ is the finite or bounded case of a conic section, the geometric shape that results from cutting a circular conical or cylindrical surface with an oblique plane . It is also the locus of all points of the plane whose distances to two fixed points add to the same constant.

Ellipses also arise as images of a circle or a sphere under parallel projection, and some cases of perspective projection.

- a. Abelian P-root group
- b. Ellipse
- c. AKS primality test
- d. ADE classification

6. In mathematics, specifically group theory, the _____ of a subgroup H in a group G is the e;relative sizee; of H in G. For example, if H has _____ 2 in G, then intuitively e;halfe; of the elements of G lie in H. The _____ of H in G is usually denoted |G : H| or [G : H].

If G and H are finite groups, then the _____ of H in G is simply the quotient of the orders of the two groups:

$$|G : H| = \frac{|G|}{|H|}.$$

By Lagrange's theorem, this number is always a positive integer.

If G and H are infinite, then the _____ of H is G is defined as the number of cosets of H in G.

a. Inner automorphism
b. Even permutations
c. Index
d. Outer automorphism

7. In mathematics, a _____ is a flat surface. Planes can arise as subspaces of some higher dimensional space, as with the walls of a room, or they may enjoy an independent existence in their own right, as in the setting of Euclidean geometry
a. -equivalence
b. -module
c. Similarity
d. Plane

8. In geometry, the foci, pronounced , are a pair of special points used in describing conic sections. The four types of conic sections are the circle, parabola, ellipse, and hyperbola.

The _____ has two equivalent defining properties; and they always fall on the major axis of symmetry of the conic.

a. Dandelin spheres
b. Derivation of the cartesian form for an ellipse
c. Conic section
d. Focus

9. A _____ is an expression which compares quantities relative to each other. The most common examples involve two quantities, but in theory any number of quantities can be compared. In mathematical terms, they are represented by separating each quantity with a colon, for example the _____ 2:3, which is read as the _____ 'two to three'.
a. Number system
b. -equivalence
c. Ratio
d. Rational number

10. In mathematics, a _____ is a series with a constant ratio between successive terms. For example, the series

$$\frac{1}{2} + \frac{1}{4} + \frac{1}{8} + \frac{1}{16} + \cdots$$

is geometric, because each term is equal to half of the previous term. The sum of this series is 1, as illustrated in the following picture:

_____ are one of the simplest examples of infinite series with finite sums.

a. 2-bridge knot
b. -module
c. -equivalence
d. Geometric series

11. In mathematics, the _____ is a conic section, the intersection of a right circular conical surface and a plane parallel to a generating straight line of that surface. Given a point (the focus) and a line (the directrix) that lie in a plane, the locus of points in that plane that are equidistant to them is a _____.

A particular case arises when the plane is tangent to the conical surface of a circle.

a. -module
b. 2-bridge knot
c. -equivalence
d. Parabola

12. The _____ are natural numbers including 0 ' href='/wiki/0_(number)'>0, 1, 2, 3, ...) and their negatives (0, −1, −2, −3, ...). They are numbers that can be written without a fractional or decimal component, and fall within the set {...
a. Abelian P-root group
b. ADE classification
c. AKS primality test
d. Integers

13. The real component of a quaternion is also called its _____ part.

The term is also sometimes used informally to mean a vector, matrix, tensor, or other usually 'compound' value that is actually reduced to a single component. Thus, for example, the product of a 1×n matrix and an n×1 matrix, which is formally a 1×1 matrix, is often said to be a _____.

a. Self-adjoint
b. Distributivity
c. Scalar
d. Tensor product

14. In mathematics, _____ is one of the basic operations defining a vector space in linear algebra Note that _____ is different from scalar product which is an inner product between two vectors.

More specifically, if K is a field and V is a vector space over K, then _____ is a function from K × V to V. The result of applying this function to c in K and v in V is denoted cv.

a. Matrix pencil
b. K-frame
c. Symplectic vector space
d. Scalar multiplication

15. In mathematics, an _____ of a product of sums expresses it as a sum of products by using the fact that multiplication distributes over addition. Expansions of polynomials are obtained by multiplying together their factors, which results in a sum of terms with variables raised to different degrees.

To multiply two factors, each term of the first factor must be multiplied by each term of the other factor.

a. Equipotential surfaces
b. Ordered vector space
c. Analytic subgroup
d. Expansion

16. In mathematics, the word _____ is a term for any well-formed combination of mathematical symbols. For example,

$x^2 + 3x - 4$

is an _____, while

)x) / 0

is not, because the parentheses are not balanced and division by zero is undefined.

Being an _____ is a syntactic concept - the meaning of the variables is irrelevant, but different fields have different notions of validity.ā€¢See formal language for how expressions are constructed, and formal semantics for meaning.

a. Unit ring
b. Expression
c. Arity
d. Orthogonal

17. In mathematics, the _____ of a real number is its numerical value without regard to its sign. So, for example, 3 is the _____ of both 3 and −3.

The _____ of a number a is denoted by $|a|$.

a. Abelian P-root group
b. ADE classification
c. AKS primality test
d. Absolute value

18. In mathematics, a _____ is a constant multiplicative factor of a certain object. For example, in the expression $9x^2$, the _____ of x^2 is 9.

The object can be such things as a variable, a vector, a function, etc.

a. Constant term
b. Coefficient
c. Tschirnhaus transformation
d. Vandermonde polynomial

19. A _____ is one of the basic shapes of geometry: a polygon with three corners or vertices and three sides or edges which are line segments. A _____ with vertices A, B, and C is denoted ABC.

In Euclidean geometry any three non-collinear points determine a unique _____ and a unique plane (i.e. a two-dimensional Euclidean space.)

a. -equivalence
b. 2-bridge knot
c. Triangle
d. -module

20. In several fields of mathematics the term _____ is used with different but closely related meanings. They all relate to the notion of mapping the elements of a set to other elements of the same set, i.e., exchanging (or 'permuting') elements of a set.

The general concept of _____ can be defined more formally in different contexts:

In combinatorics, a _____ is usually understood to be a sequence containing each element from a finite set once, and only once.

a. Rupture field
b. Binary function
c. Near-field
d. Permutation

21. A _____ is a three-dimensional solid object bounded by six square faces, facets or sides, with three meeting at each vertex. The _____ can also be called a regular hexahedron and is one of the five Platonic solids. It is a special kind of square prism, of rectangular parallelepiped and of trigonal trapezohedron.
a. Cube
b. 2-bridge knot
c. -module
d. -equivalence

22. In mathematics, a _____ is a bijection between skew diagrams satisfying certain properties, introduced by Zelevinsky (1981) in a generalization of the Robinson-Schensted correspondence and the Littlewood-Richardson rule.
a. -equivalence
b. Macdonald polynomials
c. -module
d. Picture

23. A _____, in mathematics, is a polynomial function of the form f(x) = ax^2 + bx + c = 0, where $a \neq 0$. The graph of a _____ is a parabola whose major axis is parallel to the y-axis.

Chapter 9. Sequences, Induction, and Probability

The expression $ax^2 + bx + c$ in the definition of a _____ is a polynomial of degree 2 or second order, or a 2nd degree polynomial, because the highest exponent of x is 2.

a. Vandermonde polynomial
b. Dickson polynomials
c. Factor theorem
d. Quadratic function

24. In mathematics, a _____ is any function which can be written as the ratio of two polynomial functions. _____ of degree 2 : $$y = \frac{x^2 - 3x - 2}{x^2 - 4}$$

In the case of one variable, x, a _____ is a function of the form

$$f(x) = \frac{P(x)}{Q(x)}$$

where P and Q are polynomial function in x and Q is not the zero polynomial. The domain of f is the set of all points x for which the denominator Q(x) is not zero.

a. -module
b. Legendre rational functions
c. Rational function
d. -equivalence

25. _____ is the mathematical process of putting things together. The plus sign '+' means that numbers are added together. For example, in the picture on the right, there are 3 + 2 apples--meaning three apples and two other apples--which is the same as five apples, since 3 + 2 = 5.
    a. Abelian P-root group
    b. AKS primality test
    c. ADE classification
    d. Addition

26. A _____ is a symbol that stands for a value that may vary; the term usually occurs in opposition to constant, which is a symbol for a non-varying value, i.e. completely fixed or fixed in the context of use. The concepts of constants and variables are fundamental to all modern mathematics, science, engineering, and computer programming.

Much of the basic theory for which we use variables today, such as school geometry and algebra, was developed thousands of years ago, but the use of symbolic formulae and variables is only several hundreds of years old.

a. 2-bridge knot
b. Variable
c. -equivalence
d. -module

Chapter 1
1. b   2. d   3. c   4. d   5. c   6. a   7. d   8. c   9. d   10. c
11. b   12. a   13. d   14. b   15. d   16. a   17. c   18. a   19. d   20. c
21. a   22. b   23. d   24. b   25. b   26. a   27. b   28. a   29. c   30. b
31. d   32. d   33. b   34. d   35. a   36. d   37. c   38. d   39. c   40. d

Chapter 2
1. b   2. d   3. b   4. a   5. b   6. d   7. b   8. d   9. c   10. d
11. d   12. c   13. c   14. a   15. d   16. a   17. c   18. a   19. d   20. d
21. b   22. d   23. c   24. c   25. d   26. c   27. b   28. d   29. d   30. b

Chapter 3
1. d   2. c   3. d   4. d   5. d   6. b   7. d   8. b   9. a   10. a
11. c   12. d   13. a   14. c   15. d   16. d   17. d   18. d   19. b   20. a
21. d   22. a   23. d

Chapter 4
1. b   2. c   3. d   4. b   5. d   6. d   7. a   8. d   9. d   10. d
11. d   12. c   13. a   14. c   15. d   16. b   17. d   18. d   19. d   20. b
21. a

Chapter 5
1. b   2. b   3. b   4. d   5. c   6. d   7. c   8. d   9. d   10. a
11. b

Chapter 6
1. d   2. a   3. d   4. a   5. d   6. a   7. d   8. b   9. d   10. d
11. b   12. b   13. c   14. c   15. a   16. d   17. d   18. d

Chapter 7
1. b   2. d   3. d   4. a   5. d   6. d   7. d   8. a   9. d   10. d
11. d   12. c   13. d   14. a   15. a   16. b   17. c   18. d   19. c   20. d
21. b   22. d   23. d   24. c   25. c   26. d   27. a   28. d   29. a   30. d
31. d

Chapter 8
1. b   2. a   3. d   4. d   5. d   6. c   7. c   8. d   9. a   10. a
11. a   12. d   13. c   14. a

Chapter 9
1. d   2. d   3. d   4. d   5. b   6. c   7. d   8. d   9. c   10. d
11. d   12. d   13. c   14. d   15. d   16. b   17. d   18. b   19. c   20. d
21. a   22. d   23. d   24. c   25. d   26. b

www.ingramcontent.com/pod-product-compliance
Lightning Source LLC
Chambersburg PA
CBHW081848230426

43669CB00018B/2860